FALSE GODS

Dedication

To my children and grandchildren

FALSE GODS

*Counterfeit Spirituality
in an Age of Anxiety*

*The Orthodox Answer
to the New Age Movement*

Michael Whelton

**Regina Orthodox Press
Salisbury, MA
2002**

Printed in the United States of America

ISBN: 1-928653-10-3

Regina Orthodox Press
P.O. Box 5288
Salisbury, MA 01952
1-800-636-2470
FAX: 978-462-5079

www.reginaorthodoxpress.com

CONTENTS

CONTENTS

ABOUT THE AUTHOR

Michael Whelton is an Orthodox writer whose articles have appeared in various Orthodox magazines and journals. He is also the author of the widely received *Two Paths: Papal Monarchy/Collegial Tradition,* in which he examines Rome's claims of papal supremacy in the light of the Orthodox Church, and *The Pearl: A Handbook for Orthodox Converts.*

INTRODUCTION

The inspiration for this book began when my wife and I paid a visit to a large local national book chain and were amazed at the vast selection of New Age publications. The numerous shelves almost groaned under the weight of an apparently limitless selection of titles ranging from channeling, crystal power, pyramid power, witchcraft, dream interpretation, mental telepathy, UFOs, visual imaging, reincarnation, astrology, spirit guides, etc. Christian books were dwarfed by a margin of at least ten to one. All of a sudden, I had a newfound purpose.

Over the last thirty years, the New Age movement has emerged from an underground occult–metaphysical counterculture, to become the great spiritual challenger to Christianity. It really is ironic that these incredible growths in New Age spirituality should occur at the same time trendy theologians labor in earnest to drain Christianity of its mystical, supernatural quality. In the 1980's, this movement was often dismissed as somewhat kinky and eccentric. Today, it permeates our society and is now reaching a stage of maturity—the occult has become respectable. It is a broad movement of organizations and individuals, bound together with a common, utopian vision of a brilliant new world, where an enlightened humanity will create their own reality.

Because of its multifaceted nature, the New Age movement evades precise definition, leaving many of us puzzled and mystified in coming to terms with it. However, it is my contention that the key to understanding the New Age phenomenon is twofold. First, to recognize that irrational, esoteric religious movements are as old as humanity and intensify during periods of alienation and anxiety. Second, that this is truly a Romantic movement—in its displacement of reason by intuition and emotion, its fixation with the supernatural, and the paranormal and its belief that the way to all mysteries lead inward to the human ego, bear its unmistakable marks.

The pervasive influence and attraction of this movement should be of major concern to Christians. Lorne Dawson, author *of Comprehending Cults: The Sociology of New Religious Movements* and an associate professor of sociology at the University of Waterloo, Ontario, reveals that surveys "indicate 15 percent to 20 percent of North American adults no longer practice the religion of their parents. The number who embrace major aspects of New Age philosophy without breaking from their church is even larger, approaching one third of the population." "These are the people who are refashioning what it means to be religious," he explains. "They go to church, but they're reading the Dalai Lama and *The Celestine Prophecy.*"[1] This is supported by an unpublished survey by sociologists Wade Clarke Roof and Phillip Hammond, revealing that 27 percent of Roman Catholic, Greek Orthodox, Episcopalian, and Lutheran respondents admit to a belief in astrology. Belief in reincarnation enjoyed an even higher percentage from the same respondents—31 percent.

INTRODUCTION

In the late 1960's, on a warm summer evening in Hollywood, California, my wife and I, together with some friends, lined up to see a performance of *Hair*, while the waiting crowds were entertained by street musicians and acrobats. This great musical extravaganza, that mesmerized and electrified audiences from London to Los Angeles, provided us with our first glimpse of the emerging New Age movement. The play was a celebration of man, yoga, the Hare Krishna sect, and an invitation to embrace a brave, new spiritually enlightened world—The Age of Aquarius. The theme song from the play relentlessly filled the airwaves:

> When the moon is in the seventh house, and Jupiter aligns with Mars,
>
> Then peace will guide the planets, and love will steer the stars.
>
> This is the dawning of the Age of Aquarius!
>
> Harmony and understanding, sympathy and trust abounding,
>
> No more falsehoods or derision, golden living dreams of visions, mystic crystal revelation,
>
> And the mind's true liberation. Aquarius! Aquarius! Aquarius!

Professor Johannes Aagaard of Arhus University in Denmark, a renowned expert on Hinduism, offered this observation:

INTRODUCTION

New Age really means the Aquarian Age . . .
the age of the enlightened man, the age of the
superman . . . the man with superconsciousness
has begun. . . . God is losing all importance,
man is the only thing which matters. Man is
saving himself by his knowledge, by the development of his mind faculties, by liberating himself from all the powers of his Old World and
the world of his body."[2]

The New Age movement can be divided into two
principal groups: (1) human potential, and (2) the occult, with some overlapping between the two. The human potential side uses Primal Therapy, biofeedback,
transactional analysis, sensory awareness, Gestalt
awareness, etc. The occult side—by far the more dangerous—involves crystal power, pyramid power, spirit
channeling, spirit guides, reincarnation, auras, telepathy, extraterrestrial revelations, etc.

Many Christians look at all this occult activity with
a great deal of alarm: "Aren't these people afraid of the
satanic, demonic influence?" Unfortunately, they are
not, because many of these people are several generations removed from any Christian influence, and for
those that could claim any, it is tenuous at best. Therefore, all the biblical injunctions against the occult fall on
deaf ears.

Thus far, Evangelical Protestantism has provided
the greatest response to the New Age movement—
much of it written during the latter half of the 1980's,
offering thoughtful, well-researched analysis.   There is

also a small, popular element that is shrill and sensational and points in alarm to sinister global conspiracies and the antichrist. One of the first respected Evangelicals to write about the potential danger of the New Age movement was the well-known theologian and author Francis Schaeffer. In Irving Hexam's opinion, Schaeffer

> was an acute observer of cultural trends, he correctly identified the cultural drift of contemporary Western society and sought to alert Evangelicals to what he saw as a threat to their faith. . . . Schaeffer's early criticism of what became the New Age movement remains the best Evangelical apologetic and analyses of New Age thought in print. Although he wrote in a very general style, he grasped the forces at work in modern culture and saw how intellectual ideas filtered down to the man in the street. If Evangelicals had taken note and built on the foundation Schaeffer laid, they would be in a much stronger position than is the case today.[3]

It is true that there is much in the New Age movement (which is largely drug free) that is bizarre, spiritually dangerous, irrational, and needs criticism. However, it is also true that most New Agers are intelligent, educated, well-intentioned people who are trying to cope with a massive spiritual vacuum. As Professor Michael F. Brown of Williams College comments:

> Americans who become involved in so-called New Religious Movements (NRMs) such as

8

channeling stand near the top of the nation's households with respect to income and educational attainment. . . . They hold jobs, dress presentably, establish stable loving relationships, and pay their taxes.[4]

The purpose of this book is to attempt to explore and analyze the New Age movement as a recurring phenomenon in human history and its current challenges to Christianity.

The Dark Side of the Moon: Irrationality in the Third Millennium

Materialism would not be complete without the need of now and again easing the intellectual tension, by giving way to moods of myth, by performing rites of some sort, or by enjoying with an inward lightheartedness the charms of the irrational, the unnatural, the repulsive, and, if need be, the merely silly.

—Oswald Spengler[5]

Let your mind go. Don't evaluate and don't let the left brain judge what you are thinking. Give your right brain more space. As a matter of fact, don't think.

—Shirley MacLaine[6]

On the final page of his book *Civilisation*, Lord Kenneth Clark laments the plight of post-Christian society: "The trouble is that there is still no centre. The moral and intellectual failure of Marxism has left us with no alternative to heroic materialism, and that isn't enough. One may be optimistic, but one can't be joyful at the

10

prospect before us."[7] Thus the tragic dilemma of modern man is that his materialism or material progress does not fill the deep spiritual void. For, as Kenneth Clark reminds us in his book, without spiritual vitality, civilizations inevitably decay.

To escape this arid desert and make life bearable, many people today, like the Romantics of the eighteenth century when faced with the naked materialism of the Industrial Revolution, seek refuge in irrational spirituality—enter the New Age movement. This resurgence certainly must have come as a considerable shock to those who confidently thought that the world of the occult had embarrassingly tiptoed away with all its paraphernalia in the face of a rational, technologically saturated culture. This movement is now aided by the decline of Christian influence and by a highly secularized society that has fragmented our culture, with the result that there are no longer any shared values and beliefs.

Children of Affluence

New Age religion was carried by a single generation through which it was incubated and transmitted to other parts of American society. That generation is the baby boom generation— those born between 1946 and 1964.[8]

The post-war U.S. baby boom started in 1946 and ended in 1964, producing 76 million people. The sheer enormity of this generation (one third of the population) and its difference was to guarantee societal change. In order to understand why the baby boomer generation so eagerly accepted the New Age religion, one has to return to the immediate post-war American society from which it emerged.

American serviceman returned home from the war, to a prosperous country that was now the dominant world power. The collective longing of these men returning from a long, bitter war was a family and a home. The year 1946 saw a monthly increase of 100,000 babies born per month over the previous year. The baby boomers were born into a society of unparalleled prosperity—a level of material prosperity unknown in human history. It is no exaggeration when sociologists Strickland and Ambrose claim that baby boomers were the "healthiest, best-fed, best-clothed, best-housed generation" in America's history. In 1955, the United States counted for 6 percent of the world population, producing two-thirds of the world's goods and consuming one-third of those goods. "The ranks of the impoverished were reduced by two-thirds, while the middle class rose from 13 percent of all families to a near majority of 47 percent."[9] Baby boomers were the first to experience the influence of television. In 1946, when the first boomers were born, there were only 8,000 homes with television sets. Within two years (1948), there were 100,000 homes with television sets, and by 1959, 50 million were tuned in. The baby boom generation was, therefore, the first to feel the impact of mass communications. Baby boomers were also the best-educated generation in U.S. history—90 percent graduated from high school and 50 percent had attended college, "compared to only 14 percent of their parents' generation. So baby boomers are more than twice as educated as their parents."[10]

Due to the enormous size of the baby boom generation—76 million—children in the U.S. became the center of attention; and thanks to Dr. Benjamin Spock, these children experienced very permissive upbringing. Strickland and Ambrose listed the benefits bestowed on these children by this unparalleled prosperity. Stay-at-home mothers provided full-time care, while home ownership was dramatically increased for middle- and working-class families. Employment in big corporations saw a change in the work ethic, "from hard work and self-denial to consumership; a child's peer concerns were less with adults and more with its own group; rather than parents as the sole agents of socialization, there were the mass media and peer-group influences."[11]

Because of the sheer numbers of their generation, peer pressure became an important factor with rock music as the soul for what was now the nation's first "teen culture." Because baby boomers took an ever-increasing gross national product, dispensing its cornucopia of material benefits as a birthright, their rebellion took a more idealized form—rebelling against the perceived hypocrisy of their parents' values. Since this generation comprised a third of the population, it was obvious that change was inevitable. The change, when it came, was far-reaching and fundamental in that it represented a major shift in American character.

That fundamental shift was a national preoccupation with self-fulfillment. Social analyst Daniel Yankelovich writes that, in the sixties, "the search for self-fulfillment was largely confined to young Americans on the nation's campuses."[12] By the seventies, this quest for self-fulfillment had spread to society at large, replacing strict norms of behavior with pluralism and freedom of choice. "To marry or live together; to have children early or postpone them, perhaps forever; to come out of the closet or stay in; to keep the old job or return to school; to make commitments or hang loose; to change careers, spouses, houses, states of residence, states of mind."[13]

Yankelovich further comments that in the 1970's "all national surveys showed an increase in preoccupation with self. By the late seventies, my firm's studies showed more than seven out of ten Americans (72 percent) spending a great deal of time thinking about themselves and their inner lives—this in a nation once notorious for its impatience with inwardness. The rage for self-fulfillment, our surveys indicated, had now spread to virtually the entire U.S. population. . . . Millions of Americans are hungry to live their lives to the brim, determined to consume every dish on the smorgasbord of human experience."[14] To this narcissistic cult of self-fulfillment and self-realization, the New Age movement was made to order.

A *Time* magazine cover story described the New Age movement by stating, "All in all, the New Age does express a cloudy sort of religion, claiming vague connections with both Christianity and the major faiths of the East (New Agers like to say that Jesus spent 18 years in India absorbing Hinduism and the teachings of Buddha), plus an occasional dab of pantheism and sorcery." Its inherent subjectivity, combined with the promise of immediate spiritual experience, has a magnetic appeal to citizens of a materialistic culture. "The underlying faith is a lack of faith in the orthodoxies of rationalism, high technology, spiritual law and order. Somehow, the New Agers believe, there must be some secret and mysterious shortcut or alternative path to happiness and health. And nobody ever really dies."[15]

The popularity of this major phenomenon is evidenced by the sheer number of books on sale in any large bookstore—it dwarfs Christian books by at least a five-to-one margin. As sociologist Reginald W. Bibby observes: "The size of the New Age sections in bookstores, for example, are the envy of other disciplines, including religious studies—and yes, certainly sociology."[16] In the U.S. alone, the sale of New Age books nearly doubled, from 5.6 million copies in 1992 to 9.7 million in 1995.[17] The Grammy Awards now include a special prize for New Age music.[18] As mentioned in the Introduction, Evangelical Protestantism afforded the greatest response to the New Age movement; however, much of it was written during the latter half of the 1980's, when it was still somewhat on the fringe. Today, it saturates our culture to the point that many people now openly accept beliefs and practices they would have shunned as bizarre fifteen years ago. The English poet Alexander Pope sums up this phenomenon very well:

Vice is a monster of so frightful mien,
As, to be hated, needs but to be seen;
Yet seen too oft, familiar with her face,
We first endure, then pity, then embrace.

One Toronto writer described it all as "being, well flaky, Meditation, Astrology, Tarot Cards, Reincarnation, Out-of-body-experiences, Dream analysis." Canada's *Globe & Mail* columnist Bronwyn Drainie dismissed it as being "rather like spiritual Silly Putty."[19]

This Pied Piper seductively entices millions of inwardly focused people by offering them direct religious fulfillment through the exploration of the inner space of the human ego and dispensing with commandments, creeds, and ecclesiastical authority. In order to create their own realities, New Agers have to deny absolutes, hence they jettison Christianity's inherent moral dualism (good and evil), thereby rejecting notions of right and wrong, truth or error.

The threat posed by the New Age movement has not been lost on the Roman Catholic Church. Cardinal Arinze, in an address given at the Vatican to his fellow Cardinals on April 5, 1991, alerted them of the danger:

> The rise and spread of the sects or new religious movements is a marked phenomenon in the religious history of our times. They operate with considerable vitality. Some of them are of an esoteric nature . . . they profess to offer a vision of the religious or sacred world, or means to reach other objectives such as transcendental knowledge, spiritual illumination, or self-

realization. . . . The problems and challenges thrown up by the new religious movements should be taken seriously. The Church cannot just go on with "usiness as usual."[20]

Before we explore this major cultural trend and its deep inroads into Western culture, it would be useful to look at its two most popular prophets.

The Celestine Prophecy

As evolution continues, synchronistic growth will raise our vibrations to the point where we break through to the afterlife dimension, merging that dimension with our own and ending the birth/death cycle.

— *The Celestine Prophecy: An Experiential Guide*[21]

The widespread success of *The Celestine Prophecy* speaks volumes for the spiritual state of Western society.[22] This fictional work that has been more correctly described as a New Age catechism has, for two consecutive years (in spite of widespread literary criticism), been the best-selling American hardcover book in the world. It has sold more than 8 million copies in thirty-two countries.

The author, James Redfield, was a graduate student in psychology at Auburn University in Alabama in the 60's. "It was there he began to explore the burgeoning 'third wave' theories about intuitions and psychic phenomena as part of therapy for abused children. 'For me the 60's weren't about burning down the ROTC building; they were the start of the Human Potential Movement, an explosion in research into consciousness. It was our first real breakthrough out of the materialistic paradigm.' He went to Sedona, Arizona, to explore energy vortexes; he discovered his past lives among Franciscan monks in the 16th century, among Native Americans in the 19th."[23]

Unable to find a publisher for *The Celestine Prophecy*, Redfield, in the early 1990's, published 3,000 copies himself for $13,000 by borrowing the money and depleting his life savings. Armed with a very enthusiastic endorsement from death-and-dying researcher Elizabeth Kubler-Ross ("a fabulous book about experiencing life—I couldn't put it down"), Redfield started to distribute his book. The vast New Age following snapped up 100,000 copies within a year, and Warner Books—smelling a winner—bought the title for $800,000.

The story centers on a man's search for an ancient Peruvian manuscript that is said to have been written in 600 B.C., containing nine key insights into life that promise a "massive transformation in human society." The manuscript is written in Aramaic, the Semetic language of Christ—perhaps this is supposed to infuse the document with a certain moral authority. Awkward questions such as how it got to Peru in 600 B.C. in the first place are left teasingly unanswered. In his search for the manuscript and its insights, our hero experiences numerous, fortuitous encounters that aid him in his search. The source of his help is a pantheistic energy (remember Star Wars' "the Force be with you"?) that flows through the cosmos, as our hero discovers:

> "Like this whole trip has been one coincidental event after another."

> "That begins to happen once you become alert and connected with the energy."

> "Connected?"

> "If one can connect and build up enough energy, then coincidental events begin to happen consistently."[24]

On a mountaintop, he undergoes a mystical experience of cosmic consciousness, where all existence is interwoven and his human nature melts in a vast limitless universe:

> I perceived everything to be somehow part of me. As I sat on the peak of the mountain looking out at the landscape falling away from me in all directions, it felt exactly as if I had always known as my physical body was only the head of a much larger body consisting of everything else I could see. I experienced the entire universe looking out on itself through my eyes. . . . The realization was present that my life did not, in fact, begin with my conception and birth on this planet. It began much earlier with the formation of the rest of me, my real body, the universe itself (p. 98).

CHAPTER ONE

Toward the end of the book our hero, after some harrowing experiences evading capture—written, as one critic put it, with "the narrative drive of a refrigerator maintenance manual"—reflects on the Manuscript's insights. These insights tell him that God is an impersonal force or energy indistinct from creation, and that humanity was evolving toward a higher form of life:

I knew the Manuscript's insights had finally merged in my mind into one consciousness. I was alert to the mysterious way my life evolved, as revealed by the First Insight. I knew that the whole culture was sensing this mystery again as well, and we were in the process of constructing a new world view, as pointed out by the Second. The Third and Fourth had showed me that the universe was in reality a vast system of energy and that human conflict was a shortage of and a manipulation for this energy.

The Fifth Insight revealed that we could end this conflict by receiving an inpouring of this energy from a higher source. For me, this ability had almost become habit. The Sixth, that we could clear out our old repeated dramas and find our true selves was also permanently etched in my mind. And the Seventh had set in motion the evolution of these true selves: through question, intuition of what to do, and answer. Staying in this magic flow was truly the secret of happiness.

And the Eighth, knowing how to relate in a way to others, bringing out in them the very best, was the key to keeping the mystery operating and the answers coming. . . . What was left, I knew was the Ninth, which revealed where our evolution was taking us (pp. 229–230).

This Ninth Insight propels evolution on a faster trajectory, "lifting our vibrations even higher" so that as "we humans continue to increase our vibrations, an amazing thing will begin to happen. Whole groups of people, once they reach a certain level, will suddenly become invisible to those who are still vibrating at a lower level."[25] So there we have it; the Ninth Insight offers a pantheistic paradise or nirvana where the physical body of the devotee is dissolved into the cosmos. However, our hero in his quest for the nine insights, had to overcome strong, even deadly opposition from the church hierarchy backed by the Peruvian army. A sympathetic Catholic priest explains the motive:

The manuscript is a curse. It would undermine our basic structure of spiritual authority. It would entice people to think they are in control of their spiritual destiny. It would undermine the discipline needed to bring everyone on the planet into the church, and people would be caught wanting when rapture comes (p. 237).

First of all, "rapture" is not a Roman Catholic belief or doctrine; it is pure Protestant millenarianism where, at the Second Coming of Christ, believers are transported bodily into heaven. Second, to suggest that the pseudo-mystical, pantheistic mush of the Nine Insights is capable of undermining the spiritual authority of the Church is ludicrous. However, the depressing fact is that vast numbers of people obviously do find meaning and fulfillment in this stuff—a sales clerk at a large bookstore chain informed me that many people wept over the last chapter containing the Ninth Insight. Also, witness the follow-up study guide, *The Celestine Prophecy: An Experiential Guide.*[26] The jacket of this companion volume promises to help the reader "intensify and expand the exciting knowledge contained in each of the nine insights of The Celestine Prophecy. . . . Most exciting of all, you can explore a deeper connection with your own personal energy and divine source." The jacket cover then informs us that this companion volume "is in use by study groups all over America."

Shirley MacLaine

Until mankind realizes that there is no truth, no good and there is, in truth, no evil, there will be no peace.

—Shirley MacLaine[27]

Born in Richmond, Virginia, in 1934, Shirley MacLaine, along with her brother, the future actor Warren Beatty, was raised in a strict middle-class family. Her ballet training and long-legged pixie charm propelled her to a career as a singer and dancer on Broadway. Her big break came when the leading lady in *The*

Pajama Game injured her leg, and she took over. As luck would have it, Hollywood producer Hal Wallis was in the audience and, being impressed with her performance, signed her up. A successful movie career, studded with several Academy Award nominations, quickly followed. In 1984, her brilliant performance as the grieving mother in *Terms of Endearment* finally gained for her the coveted Oscar.

In addition to her acting career, Shirley MacLaine has been passionate and outspoken on numerous causes, including civil rights, feminism, and her opposition to the Vietnam War. Her opposition to the Vietnam War required courage, because it was voiced when American public opinion was still in support of it—for this cause she clearly put her acting career on the line. While she always enjoyed a reputation as being somewhat kooky on and off screen, no one was prepared in 1983 for her third autobiography, *Out on a Limb*. Here was a book on the occult written by a famous actress with a vast, latent New Age audience waiting in the wings—it was an enormous success. The New Age movement was now part of popular culture.

In her book, Shirley MacLaine chronicles her journey, hesitant at first but then passionately embracing all the panorama of New Age occultism (e.g., channeling, spirit guides, reincarnation, astral projection, extraterrestrials and UFO's, etc.). She begins her book by describing an unabashed adulterous love affair with a British member of Parliament whom she calls Gerry Stamford. "Gerry and I never discussed his wife or my personal life. It wasn't necessary or anything we needed to get into."[28] About halfway through the book, Gerry makes his exit. The relationship fizzles out, leaving Shirley to muse about the troubled relationship they had in a previous life where "Gerry was equally devoted to his work then . . . doing important work involving cultural exchanges with the extraterrestrials."[29]

David Manning is a friend, who after overcoming Shirley's initial skepticism, leads her into the world of the occult. She has her first channeling experience with a rather eccentric young medium named Kevin Ryerson. Through him she meets several disembodied spirits (an Elizabethan Irish pickpocket named Tom McPherson, and John, who "is the most highly evolved of all the disincarnate entities" and "speaks in a biblical lingo").[30] John offers advice that is as old as man himself; offered by the serpent in the Garden of Eden:

> Man refuses to accept that he is in possession of all truth and has been from the beginning of time and space. Man refuses to accept responsibility for himself. Man is the co-creator with God of the cosmos. . . . Only when man accepts that he is part of the truth he is seeking are the truths themselves apparent."[31]

Having imparted this piece of wisdom, John then informs Shirley of her divinity and reveals the usual anti-Christian bias:

> Your world religions are on the right track basically, but they do not teach that every individual is fundamentally the creator and the controller of his own destiny. . . . It was to the

advantage of the Church to protect the people from the truth. . . . Your dogmatic religions, for example, are most limiting for mankind because they demand unquestioned reverence for authority—an exterior authority. You are God. You know you are Divine. But you must continually remember your Divinity and, most important, act accordingly.[32]

Our understanding of human sexuality and love come under attack when John informs Shirley that sex is purely gender—the deep psychological and emotional differences between men and women are denied. In fact, bisexuality enjoys a high spiritual realm in the occult world:

We are all basically the same because we have all experienced being both sexes; our souls, if you will, are basically androgynous . . . high spiritual understanding knows no sexuality differences because the elements of both sexes are simultaneously present. The polarities are evenly opposed.[33]

After sowing lies and confusion, the Romantic appeal with its inward focus, displacement of reason in favor of emotion and intuition is then urged. The problem is that when we look inward for guidance, our rich imagination can distort or destroy precise outlines and turn the finite into the infinite—our moral compass goes haywire:

You must learn to trust your feelings more and refrain from approaching so many issues in life from strictly an intellectual perspective. Intellect as a marvel is limited. Feelings are limitless. Trust your heart . . . or your intuition, as you term it.[34]

Her occultist friend David Manning takes her to Peru, where she experiences astral projection (i.e., out of body experience):

I literally felt I was flying . . . no, flying wasn't the right word . . . it was more gentle than that . . . wafting seemed to describe it best . . . wafting higher and higher until I could see the mountains and the landscape below me and I recognized what I had seen during the day. And attached to my spirit was a thin, thin silver cord that remained stretched though attached to my body.[35]

After this experience, the New Age movement had no more ardent or influential disciple than Shirley MacLaine. She ends her book with the thought that, "Maybe one day I would take a trip to the Pleiades and see what was on the other side. Would it be as full of wonder as the inner journey I was just beginning?"[36] (The Pleiades are a cluster of stars in the constellation of Taurus, referred to in Job 9:9 and 38:31: "Canst thou bind the sweet influences of Pleiades, or loose the bands of Orion?" The Pleiades are popular with New Agers as a domain for extraterrestrials.)

Shirley MacLaine's next two books, *Dancing in the Light* and *It's All in the Playing,* narrate her deepening involvement and commitment to New Age occultism. These books have sold over 5 million copies—a dramatic sign of her enormous influence. On the nights of January 18 and 19, 1987, ABC-TV produced a film dramatization of *Out on a Limb* as a two-part miniseries. Following this production, the nationwide book chain B. Dalton reported that the sales of occult books jumped by 95 percent. In their December 7, 1987, issue, *Time* magazine ran a cover story on Shirley MacLaine— New Age occultism had arrived on Main Street.

It is absolutely amazing that people find Shirley MacLaine's books believable. The sheer gullibility necessary must turn gypsy fortune-tellers green with envy. F. LaGard Smith is a professor of law at Pepperdine University in Los Angeles who wrote *Out on a Broken Limb* as an answer to Shirley MacLaine's book. Smith attended a trance session conducted by Kevin Ryerson, the medium who introduced Shirley to the world of channeled spirits. Having spent a great deal of time in England and Ireland, Smith did not find the Irish accent of the entity "Tom McPherson" convincing. During the trance session, Smith decided to test the credibility of "Tom" and his medium by falsely declaring that his mother was dead. "Tom McPherson" then replied to various questions about her as if she were alive. As Smith logically stated, "Wouldn't the Akashic Records (believed by spiritualists to be a vast scroll house stored in ethereal energy of all that has ever been) *know* whether or not my mother were still on the earth-plane?"[37]

Continuing with the charade. Smith tells the entity "Tom" that he had a dream about Shirley MacLaine and "whether a prior lifetime with Ms. MacLaine might be a possible interpretation. Sure enough, it was! Ms. MacLaine and I were associated together as collaborators in China during the eleventh century. Ms. MacLaine was a shadow puppeteer, and I was a Taoist scholar. We joined together in an effort to communicate Taoism to the people, using my scholastic knowledge and Ms. MacLaine's skills of communication through Puppeteering."[38] Smith found Kevin Ryerson to be charming and likable with "simply one of the best road shows in America."[39] My shared skepticism with Smith should not be taken as disbelief in the demonic; I, like Smith—as a fellow Christian—affirm their existence. For while direct demonic presence does not seem to be apparent, there is no doubt that Shirley and her cohorts are doing their work for them.

It is tragic that an immensely talented woman like Shirley MacLaine could be so drawn to New Age occultism and, in doing so, take perhaps millions with her. One can already see that her beliefs have unhinged her from reality: "That's my reality. So no one can say whether my reality is correct or not."[40]

Hitler's death camps and Stalin's Gulags were very much part of their reality. Are we not to pass judgment—what about the agonizing reality of the inmates?

If I created my own reality, then—on some
level and dimension I didn't understand—I had

created everything I saw, heard, touched, smelled, tasted; everything I loved, hated, revered, abhorred; everything I responded to or that responded to me. Then, I created everything I knew, I was therefore responsible for all there was in my reality. If that was true, then I was everything, as the ancient texts had taught. I was my own universe. Did that also mean I had created God and I had created life and death? Was that why I was all there was?[41]

Shirley MacLaine's obsession with the idea that we create our own reality is evidenced by her response to the following tragedy. Her daughter was heartbroken over the death of her acting teacher, who suffered a head-on collision and was burnt beyond recognition. Shirley's response was to wonder "why anyone would choose a death like that."[42] To a woman participant at one of her seminars, who described the agony of physical pain suffered since childhood, Shirley offered the following: "Sometimes people use pain to feel alive. Pain is a perception, not a reality."[43] Shirley's warped beliefs have obviously robbed her of the ability to give a human, sympathetic response to another's suffering. Perception and reality are not mutually exclusive; the vast majority of our perceptions are rooted in reality. If this were not the case, then all scientific inquiry would still be in the Stone Age.

When we consider these statements and numerous others (e.g., "I'm learning to look into the future [through mind traveling] and if I want to change it, I can"[44]), one wonders if there isn't the beginning of a psychosis in her delusions and loss of contact with reality, not to mention megalomania — "If you don't see me as God, it's because you don't see yourself as God."[45] As she drifts ever deeper into New Age occultism, one is left wondering about this poor woman's future — she needs our prayers. An equally depressing reflection are the millions of spiritually starved who find the writings of people like Shirley MacLaine and James Redfield meaningful. It is tragic that, in their spiritual quest, these authors and their vast following did not take the words of Christ to heart.

Observations

I am the Light of the world. He that followeth Me shall not walk in darkness, but shall have the light of life.

—John 8: 11

For our wrestling is not against flesh and blood; but against principalities and powers, against the rulers of the world of this darkness, against the spirits of wickedness in the high places.

—Ephesians 6:12

Christianity is not only a universal truth, it is also an historical tradition (i.e., its claims are rooted in real, historical events). It is this historical reality that separates Christianity from other religions, whose basis are purely ethical and philosophical or, like the occult, hidden. In fact, the etymology of the word *occult* means "that which is hidden." Unlike them, Christianity lives or dies on the veracity of her historical claims. For author David W. Hoover, the three distinguishing marks of the occult are:

1. The occult deals with things secret or hidden;

2. The occult deals with operations or events that seem to depend on human powers that go beyond the five senses;

3. The occult deals with the supernatural, the presence of angelic or demonic forces.[46]

It is the hidden quality of the occult that perhaps most differentiates it from Christianity, for Christianity is a "revealed" religion whose doctrine and teaching are made manifest to all. By contrast, the realm of the occult is hidden, secretive. (For example, the cover of *The Celestine Prophecy* promises its readers that "it contains secrets that are currently changing our world. Drawing on ancient wisdom, it tells you how to make connections among the events happening in your own life right now . . . and lets you see what is going to happen to you in the years to come!") This, of course, can only be acquired, not only by undergoing harrowing arduous experiences, but also being connected to an "energy force," as the hero of *The Celestine Prophecy* found in his pursuit of the Nine Insights.[47]

Another way the realm of the occult communicates its "secrets" is through a person endowed with special powers (e.g., a medium or channeler through whom disembodied spirits impart their wisdom to the likes of

Shirley MacLaine: "You are God. You know you are Divine. But you must continually remember your Divinity and, most important, act accordingly"[48]).

One of the key premises of the New Age movement is that there is no objective truth (e.g., "Until mankind realizes that there is no truth" is Satanic in its attempt to dethrone all religious and moral values). In their denial of the Christian moral duality of good and evil, New Agers are led into a quagmire of moral ambiguity. For without this necessary duality—love, justice, charity, mercy, kindness, forgiveness, hatred, cruelty, envy, etc., they lose their resolute character and drown in a relativistic quicksand. Furthermore, when New Agers commit the ultimate blasphemy by declaring, "I am God," they do not recognize any higher moral authority than themselves. This is the pride that resulted in the fall of Lucifer/Satan:

> How are you fallen from Heaven, Lucifer! Son of the Dawn! Cut down to the ground! And once you dominated the peoples! Didn't you say to yourself: I will be as high as Heaven! I will be more exalted than the stars of God! I will, indeed, be the supreme leader! In the privileged places! I will be higher than the Skies! I will be the same as the Most High God! But you shall be brought down to Hell, To the bottom of its pit. And all who see you will despise you (Isaiah 14:12–19).

Their claim that there is no objective truth is pure nonsense. For the immediate response to such an absolute statement asserting the nonexistence of truth would be to ask if that was true. Thus the silly statement ends up proving the truth it attempts to negate.

The New Age occult movement is extremely self-centered, primarily concerned with personal empowerment and what occult power will do for the individual practitioner, as America's foremost religious commentator, Martin Marty, observes:

> In all the literature there is a striking absence of positive concern for ethics, a remarkable oversight in a nation where other religions have had to prove their worth by citing their moral contributions. Except for a few attacks on unscrupulous people in their own orbit, the morality of their audience is usually assumed by these writers; it is the quality of life which will be enhanced through occult practices. But there is never a hint of interest in the use these religious insights might have in the controversial realms of social justice.[49]

CHAPTER TWO
The New Romantics

This world is a comedy to those that think, a tragedy to those that feel.

—Horace Walpole[50]

The New Age movement of today passes itself off as fresh, illuminated wisdom, giving it a trendy "with it" aura—a "cutting edge" façade, a new way of looking at things, a fresh perspective to replace our outmoded ways of thinking. However, the very opposite is true, for it is an old familiar face in human history. In the dark shadows of pre-history beyond science, beyond Christendom, beyond the humanities and the liberal arts lies the occult—the realm of hidden and forbidden knowledge. In spite of the vigilance of the Church, this "other realm" has always been a dogged, persistent fellow traveller of Christianity.

To seek meaning and significance in our existence is as fundamental to the human nature as breathing. When human beings as a society suffer anxiety, uncertainty, insecurity, and demoralization, "their attempts to provide satisfactory explanations of the human condition take on a frantic aspect. It is in such a situation of crises that the struggle for the irrational begins."[51] As in our own day, this "flight from reason" has surged periodically throughout history—in the late Roman Empire (as we shall see in the next chapter) and during the eighteenth century Enlightenment. We will explore these two eras for valuable insights.

The Age of Enlightenment

Superstition sets the whole world in flames; philosophy quenches them.

— Voltaire[52]

The great tragedy of Science — the slaying of a beautiful hypothesis by an ugly fact.

— Aldous Huxley[53]

If one were pushed to establish a starting date for the Enlightenment or the Age of Reason, then it would have to be the year 1687. This was the year when Sir Isaac Newton published his widely acclaimed *Philosophiae naturalis principia mathematica* (Mathematical Principles of Natural Philosophy), where he stated the law of universal gravitation. If human reason could penetrate and reveal the laws governing the universe, then human reason could also unlock the mysteries of nature and society, thus leading mankind into the bright, sunlit uplands of enlightenment and happiness. One of the main tenets of this cult of Reason was the naïve belief in the perfectibility of man.

With this newfound confidence in human rationality, Western society felt itself capable of sweeping away centuries of darkness, ignorance, and superstition. The secular spirit of the Enlightenment focused an intellectual skepticism on traditional Christian beliefs and dogmas; and, while it did not spell the end of religion, it did among the better-educated move it from the center of their lives to the periphery. More damaging was its effect on the clergy, for they also became caught up in the spirit of rational inquiry, with the result that the church itself became more secularized, offering little spiritual nourishment. This, combined with the increasingly mechanistic world of the Industrial Revolution, created for many people an arid, spiritual environment — reaction was inevitable.

The Romantic Movement

One only has to rid oneself of the limitations imposed by the human brain's left-hemisphere reasoning, which Western culture, by way of its technological advances, holds in such high esteem. The pathway to godhead lies not in the left hemisphere's logic but in the right hemisphere's intuitive knowing and creativeness.

— Maxine Negri.

The heart has its reasons of which reason knows nothing.

— Blaise Pascal[54]

O for a life of sensations rather than thoughts!

— John Keats[55]

Beginning with Jean Jacques Rousseau's sermons on the religion of the heart, the Romantic movement challenged the Enlightenment's claim that only science and rational analytical investigation paved the road to truth, and therefore all reality can be encompassed by the human mind. English Romantic poets such as Lord Byron, Percy Bysshe Shelley, John Keats, William Blake, and William Wordsworth contended that our inner experience of emotions and intuition also opened us to a world of truth where science and rational inquiry hold no relevance or authority. It is interesting that it was Shelley's wife, Mary, who created the Gothic thriller *Frankenstein* (1818), a hideous creature haunted with needs he has not anticipated and cannot satisfy. Norman Davies, Professor Emeritus of the University of London, comments:

> The main tenets of the Romantic movement opposed everything which the Enlightenment stood for. Where the Enlightenment had stressed the power of Reason, the Romantics were attracted by all in human experience that is irrational: by the passions, by the supernatural and the paranormal, by superstitions, pain, madness, and death. Where the Enlightenment had stressed man's growing mastery over nature, the Romantics took delight in trembling before nature's untamed might: in the terror of storms and waterfalls, the vastness of mountains, the emptiness of deserts, the loneliness of the seas. Where the Enlightenment had followed the classical taste for harmony and restraint, and for the rules which underlay civilized conventions, the Romantics courted

everything which defied established convention: the wild, the quaint, the exotic, the alien, the deranged. Where the Enlightenment had sought to expound the order underlying the apparent chaos of the world, the Romantics appealed to the hidden inner "spirits" of everything that lives and moves.[56]

Professor Davies could just have easily been describing the new Romantics (e.g., Shirley MacLaine, James Redfield, and the New Age movement). C. S. Lewis displays the close association of Romanticism and the occult in his book *Pilgrim's Regress*. He describes the land of Occultica, avoided by his Pilgrim: "The delicious tang of the forbidden and the unknown draws them (the inhabitants) on with fatal attraction: smudging of all frontiers, the relaxation of all resistances, dream, opium, darkness, death, and the return to the womb. Every feeling is justified by the mere fact that it is felt."[57]

It is interesting that, in the midst of a powerful New Age movement, the novels of Jane Austen (1775–1817) should be enjoying a surge in popularity, with film productions being made of her works *Pride and Prejudice* and *Sense and Sensibility*. Interesting, because her novels exude those classical values of the Age of Reason—moderation, balance, good sense, and restraint. For while she lived nearly half of her adult life in the nineteenth century, she was spiritually wedded to the eighteenth century and the Age of Enlightenment. Thus, Jane Austen's views and sentiments were Augustan—refined, elegant, fastidious, and gracious, which she combined with a cool feminine sense of humor. Jane Austen's attitude to the Romantic movement is captured in a scene from *Sense and Sensibility,* when the hopelessly romantic Marianne Dashwood says to her sister, "Oh, Eleanor, where are your feelings?" The response from her elder sister is curt, "I govern them."

To a Romantic writer such as Charlotte Bronte (author of *Jane Eyre)* the sense of moderation, balance, and restraint as evidenced in Jane Austen's Emma aroused criticism. "What sees keenly, speaks aptly, moves flexibly, it suits her to study, but what throbs fast and full, though hidden, what the blood rushes through, what is the unseen seat of Life and the sentient target of death—this Miss Austen ignores."[58]

New Age and Mainstream Culture

Our stance is that people are unlimited in their individual abilities, that as humans all of us are able to do anything we want . . . [and] that all of us desire to express a greater wholeness and to be consciously in charge of our lives.

—Chris Majer, *Sportsmind*[59]

There are no victims in this life or any other. No mistakes. No wrong paths. No winners. No losers. Accept that and then take responsibility for making your life what you want it to be.

—Jack Underhill[60]

Your discoveries are your truth without need-
ing outside validation.

— Esalen Institute[61]

As I mentioned in the Introduction, the New Age is
a broad movement of organizations and individuals,
bound together with a common utopian vision of a
brilliant new world. A sign of its increasing maturity is
its widespread penetration of our culture. Comprising
not only of individuals but "activist groups, businesses,
professional groups, and spiritual leaders and followers, the movement brought feminist, ecological, spiritual, and human-potential concerns into the
mainstream in the 1980's. Thus creating a large market
in the United States and other countries for books,
magazines, audio and videotapes, workshops, retreats,
and expositions on the subject, as well as for natural
foods, crystals, and meditation and healing aids. Techniques for self-improvement and the idea that the individual is responsible for, and capable of everything
from self-healing to creating the world, have found ap-
plications in health care and counseling as well as in
sports, the armed forces, and corporations."[62]

There is a $50 million market in the subliminal self-
help audio and videotapes. I frequently hear them on
my car radio, offering everything from effortlessly im-
proved memory to self-esteem. They work, according to
one manufacturer, because "subliminal messages by-
pass the conscious mind, and imprint directly on the
subconscious mind (even during sleep) where they create the basis for the kind of life you want." This, of

course, is pure New Age dogma that insists that we all possess a dormant unlimited potential that can be released if we apply the right stimuli—yes, even subliminal tapes. However, various tests have concluded that subliminal self-help tapes do not confer any demonstrable value to the user.[63]

In 1995, the U.S. government declassified secret records that revealed that during the early 1970's, the United States Central Intelligence Agency funded a program to see if extrasensory perception (ESP), euphemistically called "remote viewing," possessed any value in the spy trade. This program not only involved laboratory studies at the Stanford Research Institute, but also employed psychics to concentrate on particular areas of interest to the CIA. Ultimately, the CIA did not consider the psychics to be very promising sleuths, as they cancelled the project in the late 1970's. The Defense Intelligence Agency, however, proved to be more optimistic in the psychics' ability and continued to fund the project until disillusionment caused withdrawal of support in 1995.[64] It appears, however, that the CIA did not only rely on psychics, for "it has been reported from various inside sources that the CIA has on occasion tried, through mediums, to contact the spirits of its dead agents. The purpose, of course, was to find out who had betrayed them, and what secrets they may have learned or divulged under torture that had not been reported prior to their deaths."[65]

Equally bizarre is the reliance on psychics by numerous police departments on both sides of the Atlantic—up to 35 percent of urban police departments in the

U.S., with widespread use in Britain, Holland, Germany, and France.[66] For instance, the New York police "have quietly sought the supernatural assistance of Ms. Allison on several investigations, from the case of a dead child found along the Bronx parkway to that of a college student who vanished one night from the Upper East Side. Investigators often give her crime-scene photographs of corpses to help her concentrate." On one occasion, her visions sent more than a dozen police officers and FBI agents on a two-day intensive dig in a Brooklyn lot. Ms. Allison persuaded them that they would find the body of a police officer's wife. Their efforts only produced the remains of two dogs.[67]

Numerous studies have concluded that the ability of psychics in police investigation work is dubious, at best. In 1979, the Los Angeles Police Department initiated a study conducted by Reiser, Ludwig, Saxe, and Wagner involving twelve psychics. Several sealed envelopes were handed to the psychics containing physical evidence from four crimes (two solved, two unsolved). Only after being requested to visualize the crimes that had occurred were they permitted to open the sealed envelopes and offer any additional impressions they received from the material. "The study was double-blind, as neither the psychics nor the experimenters had any prior knowledge of the details of the crimes. The psychics' performances were less than impressive. For example, the experimenters knew that 21 key facts were true of the first crime. The psychics identified an average of only 4. Similarly, of the 33 known facts concerning the second crime, the psychics correctly identified an average of only 1.8. This data caused Reiser *et al.* to conclude that 'The research data does not support the contention that psychics can provide significant additional information leading to the solution of major crime.'"[68]

With such a dismal track record, the question arises as to why the police use them? "There is a tangle of reasons why detectives from what may be the country's best police departments reach out to a psychic. When distraught families beg them to inject the paranormal into cases of the dead and missing, the police find it hard to say no."[69]

New Age and Corporate America

One of the stranger spin-offs of the New Age movement has been the adoption of many of its tenets by the business world. There have always been a few executives who consulted their astrologers before making important business decisions. But today many of the questionable New Age practices have been adopted and installed by companies as part of their operations.[70]

Of all the myriad organizations within the New Age movement, there is no doubt that the human potential movement has achieved the greatest cultural penetration, a penetration significantly aided by a corporate America that shells out $4 billion annually on human potential training courses.[71] According to the *New York Times*, "One concept commonly transmitted in the sessions by 'human potential' groups is that because man is a deity equal to God he can do no wrong; thus there is no sin, no reason for guilt in life."[72] Over 50 percent of Fortune 500 corporations have exposed their employees to some form of New Age human potential training (e.g., AT&T, General Motors, Ford, IBM, Calvin Klein, Westinghouse, Dupont, Scott Paper, Campbell Soup, Lockheed, RCA, Proctor and Gamble, All State Insurance, NEC, Boeing Aerospace, General Foods, General Electric, and McDonalds).[73] This was confirmed by a revealing article, which appeared in the September 28, 1986, edition of the *New York Times:*

> The magazine *California Business* reported recently that its survey of 500 company owners and presidents found more than half said they had resorted to some form of 'conscious raising' technique. Although such 'human potential' programs are more common in California than elsewhere, industry experts say that recently they have been the fastest growing type of executive development program.

Stanford University's Graduate School of Business Professor Michael Ray authored a book entitled *Creativity in Business,* which includes meditation, chanting, "dream work," the use of tarot cards, discussion of the "New Age Capitalist," and "even specific instructions on how to contact a personal "Spirit Guide."[74] Ray says that "it's not that unusual these days to see enormously successful, hard-core corporate types doing biofeedback and using crystals." Among the more celebrated speakers at Ray's business course have been Apple Computer co-founder Steven Jobs and Discount Broker Charles Schwab.[75]

Representatives of some of the nations largest corporations, including IBM, AT&T, and General Motors, met in New Mexico in July to discuss how metaphysics, the occult, and Hindu mysticism might help executives compete in the marketplace.[76]

The underlying premise of the human potential movement is its unabashed pantheism (Greek *pan*, "all," and *Theos*, "God"). Pantheism asserts that God is not a Being with personality who contemplates His creation from the outside. Rather, God is only identifiable with the forces of nature, thus the infinite demarcation between the Creator and His creation dissolves into a cosmic oneness—All is God, All is One. ("'I am God,' shouts Shirley MacLaine on the Malibu beach".[77]) The English poet Alexander Pope (1688–1744) described pantheism in an exquisitely phrased passage in his *Essay on Man:*

> All are but parts of one stupendous whole,
> Whose body Nature is, and God the soul;
> That chang'd thro' all, and yet in all the same,
> Great in the earth, as in th' aethereal frame.

In their pantheistic world, New Agers believe that God is nothing more than an impersonal force or energy contained within creation—everything is God. With the abolition of a Christian transcendent God, the German philosopher Friedrich Nietzsche warned: "When one gives up the Christian faith, one pulls the right to Christian morality out from under one's feet."[78]

For with the "death of God" comes the death of morality and the death of truth, with the result that the concept of good and evil disappear. Only personal values remain and, like Nietzsche's "new man," New Agers with their self-appointed divinity debase virtues into values. They are then free to trans-valuate them into their own "personal" values. The mere creature now becomes the creator, and with the help of the human potential movement, they can create their own reality and realize their unlimited potential.

Former astronaut Brian O'Leary's journey of self-awareness and self-discovery started when he attended a Lifespring seminar held by New Age consultants:

> Seven years ago I took a Lifespring training in Philadelphia, and it awakened parts of me that I never knew existed. Then I took an Insight training and began studying MSIA (Movement of Spiritual Inner Awareness) discourses about two years ago, and I've been sailing ever since...
>
> During a spiritual retreat, I reconnected with a feeling . . . which I knew had to come from inside myself . . . . I just knew that outer space was a manifestation of inner development. . . .
>
> Outer space for me is a physical metaphor for inner space. . . . There is so much . . . we can do to accelerate the new age.[79]

At one time the U.S. Surgeon General's office declared that Lifespring "has considerable potential for emotional harm."[80]

New Age psychotherapist Jean Houston is a co-director of Mind Research in New York. She claims, "Our minds are stargates, our bodies celled of mystery, which when unraveled, give us citizenship in a world larger than our aspiration, more complex than all our dreams."[81] Houston uses a technique called "regressing," whose underlying premise is reincarnation and evolution. By parodying the evolutionary process, Jean Houston attempts to unburden a group of Sacramento citizens of their "submerged memories" and discover their true inner selves:

> "Remember when you were a fish," Houston suggested in Sacramento. Nearly a thousand people . . . dropped to the floor and began moving their "fins" as if to propel themselves through water.
>
> "Notice your perceptions as you roll like a fish. How does your world look, feel, sound, taste? Then you come up on land," Houston recalled, taking us through the amphibian stage. . . .
>
> Then Houston suggested, "Allow yourself to fully remember being a reptile. . . . Then some of you flew. Others climbed trees." . . . We became a zoo of sounds and movements made by early mammals, monkeys, and apes. Houston then called us to remember being "the early humans" who loses his/her "protective furry covering" and . . . evolves into the modern human.

The climax of the already intense exercise that had taken us more than an hour followed: "Now I want you to extend yourselves even further — into . . . the next stage of your evolution." We became a room of leaping, joyous, sometimes alone, often together human beings who eventually joined hands and voices. The impact was electric. . . .

We had become a wriggling sea of bodies — nearly a thousand housewives, therapists, artists, social workers, clergy, educators, health professionals . . . [who] had crawled over and under each other, enjoying ourselves and re-learning what was deep within our memories.[82]

The above scene reminds me of an observation made by the late English writer and commentator Malcolm Muggeridge that "reality is the bane of comedians." As editor of the British humor magazine *Punch*, Muggeridge would meet once a week with the magazine's assistant editors and writers and survey the political and social scene, in order to create satire. He lamented, however, to being constantly confronted with the "tragic dilemma of how to ridicule a world whose reality so often outdoes their wildest and most daring inventions."[83]

Pete Saunders, head of Success Potentials Unlimited, a human potential consulting firm, admits that the "psychic foot in the door" to corporate America has been stress management. "Business equated psychic with weird . . . but they understood stress and . . .

needed help with that. When they saw how effective our mental dynamics worked for stress they said, 'Give us more.' So now you talk about psychic attunement and expanded mental states, and they say, 'How can I use that in my business?'"[84]

One of the most successful human potential seminars with a high profile celebrity following is est, founded by Werner Erhard (born Jack Rosenberg) in 1971. Est gained a great deal of notoriety for its radical methods and outright intimidation in inducing trainees to "get it" (i.e., overcoming their personal problems or obstacles). Essentially, est pupils are taught that we all create our own reality and are, therefore, entirely responsible for the reality in which we find ourselves. Est insists that the pathway to happiness and success lies in the ability to change our reality. That is "getting it."

One of the more esoteric New Age corporate training seminars has to be California-based Insight Seminars, which is part of the Movement for Spiritual Inner Awareness (MSIA). John-Roger Hinkins — or just plain John-Roger, as he prefers — is the self-proclaimed ambassador of the Mystical Traveller Consciousness, a spiritual being who appears in many incarnations and is able to reveal the divinity hidden in all of us. To preach this good news to the employees of corporate America, MSIA launched Insight Seminars in 1978. Before the first Insight meeting, John-Roger called together the seminar leaders and revealed to them that he had just returned from a four-day meeting on a Hawaiian mountaintop. In attendance were "the spiritual hierarchy of the planet" (e.g., Jesus, Krishna, and other "ascended masters").[85]

John-Roger informed his seminar leaders "that the new Insight program would provide them with an opportunity to 'look at the teachings of the Traveler . . . in a different perspective.'" At the beginning of each Insight training session, the trainers and assistants would purify themselves and the room by "calling in the Light," repeating the following:

> Father–Mother God, we ask just now to be placed in the light of the Holy Spirit, through John-Roger, the Mystical Traveller, Preceptor of Consciousness, and we ask only that for which is for the highest good be brought forth.[86]

Big-name employers such as Lockheed, McDonnell Douglas, Chemical Bank, the U.S. Social Security Administration, and Scott Paper were eager to sign up their employees. One graduate of an Insight Seminar gushed: "It gave me a sense of purpose and clarity about my life. . . . It was magical, an incredible high."[87]

In 1984, Richard Watring, personnel director for Budget Rent-a-Car, mailed 9,000 questionnaires to personnel directors in the United States, requesting them to indicate which of the following New Age techniques they found "particularly effective." These were Focusing, Silva Mind Control, Meditation, Hypnosis, Est, Dianetics, Transcendental Meditation, Biofeedback, Centering, Imagery, and Yoga. (See glossary of terms below.) Of the 856 respondents, 111 (14 percent) claimed at least one of the eleven techniques as being effective. The most popular technique proved to be Biofeedback, with 5 percent believing in its effectiveness. Around 45 percent of the respondents admitted to exposing their employees to one or more of these techniques.

Watring concludes that "this illustrates a significant level of acceptance and use of these 'New Age' concepts." Watring also found that those who believe the use of New Age techniques (or "psychotechnologies") are effective for human-resource management have a greater tendency to believe New Age presuppositions than those who do not.[88] Watring further added that "private corporations that are not church-affiliated should neither attempt to change the basic belief systems of their employees nor should they promote the use of techniques (i.e. altered consciousness) that accelerate such change; and while spiritual growth is important, corporations should not prescribe the methods whereby employees grow spiritually. This is better left for those more qualified than the human resource development department."[89]

A number of U.S. corporations have encountered stiff resistance from their employees in implementing human potential training programs. One of the more celebrated cases involved California's Pacific Bell's introduction in 1987 of the Krone Training for its 67,000 employees, at a cost of $160 million. Part of the training required employees to deliberate on the possibility of "a purpose that is beyond self." Critics were quick to point out that this was nothing more than an entrée into universal unity consciousness—a New Age concept. The training sessions were conducted by associates of Charles Krone—a disciple of the Russian mystic Georges Gurdjieff. Hundreds of employees complained that "the training was based on spiritual philosophies not appropriate in a job setting."

The California Public Utilities Commission conducted an investigation and ruled "that PacBell stockholders, rather than consumers, must pay $25 million of the estimated $160 million total cost of the training. In addition, employees sent to training seminars which caused them serious psychological or even physical injury may claim damages from their employer as well as the trainers if attendance was mandatory, either explicitly or implicitly." PacBell cancelled the Krone program (15,000 of its 67,000 employees had already taken it) and conducted its own study.[90]

A major petrochemical company is providing its employees with routine workshops in stress management, which includes a faith healer to "read auras for ailing employees and run her hands over their fields of energy."[91]

Holistic health has proven to be a major challenger to traditional Western medical science—especially in the field of preventative medicine. The Association for Holistic Health asserts that their approach is "person oriented rather than disease oriented," enjoying "full vibrant health (positive wellness), not symptom amelioration" as its goal and aiming for "primary prevention rather than crises intervention."[92] Traditional medicine has a brilliant record in acute care, invasive surgery (e.g., open-heart surgery, organ transplants, hip replacements, reattaching severed limbs, etc.), and producing wonder drugs. Unfortunately, this brilliant record is not duplicated in the area of preventative health, and it is this vacuum that holistic health has largely filled. Holistic health addresses the whole person (i.e., physical, emotional, and spiritual), an approach Western medicine has long forgotten in its reductionistic approach, viewing the patient only in terms of isolated body parts.

While there is a great deal of good in holistic health, there is also an equal amount of quackery and spiritual danger. On the positive side, it has filled an obvious void in Western medicine with its focus on the whole person, "primary prevention," and encouraging people to be more responsible and assertive with their own health, rather than passively relying on chemical drugs and crises surgical intervention. On the negative side, a Christian has to realize that many of its practices are based on the principle that there is a spiritual energy, or force, flowing through the cosmos and every human being. This impersonal energy or force is called the "Divine Force" or "God" — a far cry from the caring, personal Christian God of the Bible. This energy or force is pure Eastern mysticism, and it is this Eastern mysticism that permeates much of the New Age holistic health movement. Hence, "pain is understood not as a symptom but as an accumulation of energy in some part of the body, which, if correctly redistributed, can restore health and harmoniously 'balance' the body. 'Energy — psychic energy — corrects or balances organic wrongness.'"[93] Here we have the favorite principle of mind over matter.

Some of the more questionable holistic health practices employing this Eastern vision and other esoteric beliefs are as follows:

Accupressure: Also known as Shiatsu, believes that healing can be achieved by redirecting energy flows within the body by applying pressure to particular points of the body.

Acupuncture: A 3,000-year-old Chinese practice that claims to redirect energy flows by inserting needles at specific points in the body to relieve everything from stress, pain, substance abuse, etc. Its critics are numerous.

Aromatherapy: Dr. Bach, a British physician and scientist, formulated essential oils from 38 flowers and trees in order to treat stress. This treatment has now been expanded to address skin disorders, immune deficiencies, and infections.

Biofeedback: Electronic instrumentation monitors physiological behavior and displays the information back to the patient on meters and light responsive equipment. The patients are then taught to "take control" of their body's functioning in lowering blood pressure, body temperature, and heart rate to relieve tension and stress. It is also claimed to be efficacious for irritable bowel syndrome, asthma, and epilepsy.[94]

Crystals: "Healing yourself with crystals" is one of the more bizarre holistic health practices. Crystals are believed to convey and project cosmic energy, thus "it is so very important that the stones which we choose and use should 'vibrate' on a frequency as close as possible to our own" and then "by simply wishing—or visualizing—the crystaline energy to be used in a particular way—it will be! It really is that simple."[95]

New Age guru Shirley MacLaine is fastidiousness personified when it comes to aligning her crystals, "I checked the positions of my four quartz crystals sitting on each corner of the tub. I had been learning to work with the power of crystals, and that discipline had become part of my daily life."[96] It is claimed that there are few human ailments—indeed very few—that lie beyond the crystals power to heal.

Electromagnetic Healing: The belief here is that chemical imbalances can upset the body's bioelectrical or energy system, causing ill health. Electromagnetic therapy seeks to restore equilibrium by using electromagnetic instruments that are applied to the patient.

Energy Medicine: Energy medicine bills itself as being able to heal a wide variety of illnesses by the emission of unseen energy, from one person to another.

Guided Imagery: The power of the mind can stimulate a person's immune system by creating mental pictures of the body fighting back and overcoming a wide range of diseases and conditions.

Iridology: The iris of the eye in its color, structure, and markings reveals any stresses and weaknesses present in a patient, including the condition of all vital organs.

Reflexology: This practice insists that there are points on the hands and feet that are linked to the major glands and organs of the body. Therapy is achieved by massaging the area of the hand or foot that corresponds to the afflicted part of the body.

Yoga: Originally one of six systems of Indian Hindu philosophy and based on a very fanciful theory of human physiology. Beginning at the base of the spine, there are (in ascending order) seven chakras or wheels of psychic power, culminating at the top of the head with *sahasrara*, the supreme center of psychic power. Yoga attempts to arouse the dormant divine power, or force, existing in these seven chakras or wheels by various exercises and mental disciplines. Ultimately, the Yoga devotee seeks to bring the physical body under the control of the mind.

While writing this chapter, our local weekly paper was delivered to our door, announcing the grand opening in our small town of a New Age shop called "Mystical Moments." This new shop, we are informed, "will offer healing services, massage therapy, tarot card readings, and products such as herbs, gem stones, second-hand metaphysical books and used altar supplies like candle holders, which" — we are assured — "will be cleansed of their inharmonious energies" — one wonders how that is done. The article comes replete with a photo of the proprietress seated demurely in her "Stargate" meditational device. She comments that "People are moving away from structured religion" and "urges people to listen to their hearts and follow their intuitions"[97] — a true Romantic.

Observations

For the scientist who has lived by his faith in the power of reason, the story ends like a bad dream. He has scaled the mountains of ignorance, he is about to conquer the highest peak; as he pulls himself over the final rock, he is greeted by a band of theologians who have been sitting there for centuries.

—Robert Jastrow, Director of NASA's Goddard Institute[98]

The Romantics of the Enlightenment, of course, were right in challenging the arrogance of science that only empirical evidence (relying on only experimental evidence) offers real truth. As Christians, we would join the Romantics in asserting that love, justice, mercy, charity, and forgiveness, while not being three-dimensional objects that can be weighed and analyzed in a laboratory, are nevertheless true. It should also be pointed out that the very basis of all scientific inquiry is founded on a philosophical insight that cannot be proven empirically (i.e., "Every becoming demands a cause"). This is a philosophical insight—pure philosophy—that no laboratory experiment can prove.

One might respond that this is surely common sense—things just don't happen by themselves. Well, it might be to us in our post-industrial, highly technical society, but for many cultures throughout history, things just happen and that's that. It was Western man, namely the early Greek philosophers, who asserted that there is a sufficient cause to occurrences, thus giving birth to Western science.

As Christians, we can never assent to the authority of reason over revelation — finite human reason comes to a standstill before the mystery of the infinite God. Besides, reason alone is impotent in laying down moral sanctions. As Professor Gerald R. Cragg points out:

> After twenty-five years of revolutionary tur-moil and warfare, Europe decided that the fruits of this philosophy were discord, violence, and disillusionment. Consequently, a resolute attempt was launched to overthrow the self-evident certitudes which had seemed so decep-tively obvious to the Age of Reason. If for no other reason, the philosophy of reason must be wrong because it had lost its moral bearings. Reason could dissolve the basis of religious faith, but it could provide no comparably satis-fying sanction for good behaviour.[99]

On the spiritual level, Christians and New Age devotees are worlds apart. The common shared under-lying premise of New Agers is Monism – *mono* meaning "one" — which states the belief "that all is one," which is pure occult philosophy. All life and inanimate matter is derived from a single energy source or force. Thus, they deny any duality of mind or matter, good or evil, and reduce all reality to a single, unifying principle. This is diametrically opposed to the Christian biblical view of God as a distinct personal being who presides over the separateness and diversity of His creation. For, as Orthodox Christians, we are reminded in the Divine Liturgy that we all stand as individuals "before the dread judgment seat of Christ." We will not be able to dissolve and hide our souls or deeds in some giant cosmic soup.

This Monism and its close ally, Pantheism, permeate the human potential movement that caters to corporate America. Joel Latner, in *The Gastalt Therapy Book,* states that: "Questions of goodness and morality . . . are superfluous. The issue is whether we shall realize our possibilities or deny them."[100] In other words, you give yourself license "to do your own thing." "A deeper presupposition must also be questioned, one that fuels the entire human potential and New Age enterprise, namely, the inherent goodness of the self. Human potential and transpersonal thought assume the unity of the self with the All, which conveys to the self, power, and authority. Oneness with the One is good for the self, and the experience of the One leads to self-actualization. Evil is simply ignorance of one's true potential and a frustration of the natural drive toward self-actualization."[101]

On the romantic attraction of Pantheism and its vision of an all-encompassing divine unity, Christian writer Abraham Kuyper wrote:

> Pantheistic ferment is deeply rooted in our sinful desires. The waters of pantheism are sweet, their religious flavor is particularly pleasant. There is spiritual intoxication in this cup, and once inebriated the soul has lost its desire for the sober clearness of the divine Word. To es-

cape from the witchery of these pantheistic charms, one needs to be aroused by bitter experience. And once awakened, the soul is alarmed at the fearful danger to which this siren had exposed it.[102]

The English poet Samuel Taylor Coleridge echoed these same sentiments when he became suspicious of the pantheism in the works of fellow poet William Wordsworth. In later life, he wrote how he had been "intoxicated with the vernal fragrance and effluvia from the flowers and first-fruits of Pantheism . . . unaware of its bitter root."[103]

CHAPTER THREE

The Spiritual Vacuum of Ancient Rome

I conjure you up, holy beings and holy names; join in aiding this spell, and bind, enchant, thwart, strike, overturn, conspire against, destroy, kill break Eucherius, the charioteer, and all his horses tomorrow in the circus at Rome. May he not leave the barriers well; may he not be quick in the contest. . . . May he meet with an accident; may he be bound; may he be broken; may he be dragged along by your power, in the morning and afternoon races. Now! Now! Quickly! Quickly!

—Curse by Enchantment[104]

The New Age phenomenon is a Romantic, irrational movement that has a long pedigree in human history. In tracing the history of irrational, esoteric religious movements in Western culture, we should not overlook the spiritual state of the late Roman Empire and the West of 2,000 A.D. as the parallels are too obvious to ignore.

Over a period of 500 years, the city of Rome grew from its seven small hills on the Tiber into a vast empire that encompassed much of the known world. As one poet expressed it, Rome had "made one City, where there was once a world." The cities and towns of the Roman Empire teemed with citizens from its four corners (e.g., Greeks, Syrians, Egyptians, Germans, Gauls, North Africans, etc.). It created the world's first multicultural society with the same social stresses and strains that we experience today. One contemporary writer, on observing numerous Syrian and Egyptian migrants pouring into Rome, wrote that "The Orontes (which flows through Lebanon) now flows through the Tiber."[105]

The religion of early Rome was one of external form and ritual — a communal affair with little or no emphasis on a spiritual, internal experience. The Romans' relationship with their gods was a legalistic relationship of promises and favors — their prayers permeated with the phrase *do ut des* — "I give so that you may give."[106] For instance, the Roman statesman Cato's "instructions for the propitiatory rituals to be carried out on farms were delivered in the tone of an agricultural bulletin"[107] exemplifies this businesslike manner toward the gods. While external ritual persisted in public life, the new global culture with its growing rootless society slowly cut Romans adrift from "the old verities that had provided a sense of security and place. In the search for a transcendent connection, the pre-Christian world turned away from traditional gods."[108] Besides, a religion that did not command and inspire virtue and morality was spiritually shallow.

This religious indifference is eloquently recorded in a letter written by the Roman statesman and orator

Marcus Tullius Cicero to his wife as he journeyed into foreign exile:

> If these miseries are to be permanent, I only wish my dearest, to see you as soon as possible and to die in your arms, since neither gods, whom you have worshipped with such pure devotion, nor men, whom I have always served, have made us any return.[109]

Oxford University's Charles Norris Cochrane, in his seminal work, *Christianity and Classical Culture*, describes the end results of this spiritual vacuum:

> Thus . . . the last shreds of traditional restraint had been contemptuously flung aside, and the dominant note was one of individual freedom and self-assertion. Inflamed by an insatiable thirst for novel forms of experience, members of the aristocracy let themselves go in a protracted orgy of extravagance and debauchery. The world was ransacked to provide the rarest and most exotic means for the satisfaction of the senses, and the last refinements of luxury and vice were introduced to titillate appetites already jaded by pleasure in its cruder forms. A literature of lyric poetry grew up which reflected only too vividly the prevailing atmosphere, and Catullus and others survive to bear witness to the sophistication and decadence of the imperial city. . . . Nor was the epidemic confined to the more exalted circles of imperial society. Among the masses, bread and circuses on

a rapidly expanding scale afforded a counter-part to the Lucullan banquets of the rich . . . if, indeed, we may trust the sober and judicious observation of Seneca, this was the climax of a materialism which brought with it a speedy nemesis in the utter demoralization of Roman life. High and low alike, without distinction of age, rank, or sex, the Romans indulged in a riot of sensationalism and emotionalism which . . . promoted social disintegration.[110]

Accompanying this spiritual vacuum was a "break-down of rationalism and the scientific spirit"[111] —a de-cline from the lofty critical rationalism of Plato and Aristotle to one of superstitious credulity. "Oracular sayings circulated more widely, prophets spoke more often in the marketplace, magical feats were more credulously studied and imitated, and the restraints of common reason became a little less common, decade by decade, even among the highly educated."[112] This was fertile soil for astrology and the mystery religions of the East that could so readily respond to "the growing spiritual anxiety, which the orthodox religion of Rome neither recognized nor catered for."[113]

Astrology and Magic

The birth of Philoe. Year 10 of the Lord Antoni-nus Caesar, Phamenoth 15 to 16, first hour of the night. Sun in Pisces, Jupiter, and Mercury in

Aries, Saturn in Cancer, Mars in Leo, Venus and Moon in Aquarius, horoscope Capricorn.

—Roman horoscope, A.D. 150[114]

If we are but instruments of heavenly rotations, then we do not have free will. And if mankind loses freedom, it loses everything.

—St. Gregory of Nyssa[115]

Why is there such a diversity in the life of twins, in their actions, fortunes, deeds, callings, honors, and all such things pertaining to human life; is this the result of a tiny interval of time, even though they were conceived in the same moment?

—Blessed Augustine[116]

"With the victory of astrology, irrationalism, and the Eastern Mystery religions over the minds of men . . . the eclipse of ancient science was complete."[117] Under these societal conditions, the rational spirit in the Roman Empire underwent a complete collapse, "and in its place came widespread superstition and a conviction of fatalism in human affairs. In this milieu astrology attained its greatest vogue in history, dominating all levels of society, even the best minds, with supreme authority."[118] Astrology, with its belief that human affairs are decisively influenced by the planets and the stars, was the chief attraction to those who found the mystery religions unappealing. Stoic philosophy, with its doctrine of the infallibility of fate guiding human destiny, offered astrology a strong endorsement.

The intrinsic, irresistible fatalism in astrology leads, by necessity, to a suffocating determinism where all events and human actions are determined by causes external to the human will. This obviously has a ruinous effect on a person's relationship with their respective gods, for if human affairs were truly dominated by the fatal power of the stars, there was little point in petitioning the gods.

For the Romans, "magic offered a way of escape from the iron compulsion of astrological fate. It undertook by secret practices to bring into service of man both the power of the stars and all the good and evil forces of the universe. The magical books of antiquity and the numerous extant magical papyri give an instructive glimpse into that world in which primitive human instincts, fear of the obscure and incomprehensible in nature and in human events, hatred of fellow-men, delight in sensation, the thrill of the uncanny all find unrestrained expression."[119] An example of "hatred of fellow-men" is the malice-filled Curse by Enchantment found at Rome. It was written about 75–40 B.C.:

> O wife of Pluto (god of the underworld), good and beautiful Proserpina (unless I ought to call you Salvia), pray tear away from Plotius health, body, complexion, strength, faculties. Consign him to Pluto your husband. May he be unable to avoid this by devices of his. Consign that

man to the fourth-day, the third-day, the every-day fever (malaria). May they wrestle and wrestle it out with him, overcome and over-whelm him unceasingly until they tear away his life. So I consign him as victim to thee, Pro-serpina, unless, O Proserpina, unless I ought to call thee Goddess of the Lower World. . . . Should there so exist any written curse, great or small—in what manner Plotius has, according to the laws of magic, composed any curse and entrusted it to writing, in such manner I con-sign, hand over to thee, so that thou mayest consign and hand over that fellow in the month of February. Blast him! Damn him! Blast him utterly! Hand him over, consign him, that he may not be able to behold, see, and contemplate any month further![120]

As a popular superstition, astrology has had a per-sistent checkered past. In the Classical world, it enjoyed enormous popularity and influence. However, with the rise of Christianity, the determinism of astrology clashed with the Christian doctrine of free will, which sent it into a long, slow decline until "the dawn of the nineteenth century, when astrology became an ex-ploded superstition."[121]

With the birth of the New Age movement, astrol-ogy is undergoing a spectacular renaissance. According to sociologist Shoshanah Fehrer, women are over-represented in the New Age movement. This, she rea-sons, is due to the intuitive nature of women, "a charac-teristic held in high esteem by New Agers." Fehrer goes on to explain how the New Age movement gives women a sense of power. Some consider New Age spirituality to be essentially feminine, thus giving them a power not enjoyed by men. In this way, women's spirituality is empowering. "It allows women to take control of their lives. . . . Wherever there are feminist communities, women are reexploring psychic phenomena that advocate personal control: astrology, Tarot, pre-patriarchal forms of religion, goddess-centered philosophies, ESP, etc. Astrology, for example, allows women to look within themselves by helping to

> develop a new understanding of our universe and how we operate in it. . . . This knowledge is power, power enabling a woman to sense her own uniqueness, to become aware of her strengths and weaknesses, and to take control of her own identity. . . . To claim her own definition—that these qualities, whatever they may, are her own and can be changed or controlled by no one but herself—is real empowerment.[122]

It is a rare supermarket checkout counter that does not have a rack of little monthly booklets offering horoscopes for your particular sign. One such publication, in its July, August, September 2000 edition, offers some titillating news for those born under the sign of Taurus: "With Venus as Taurus' ruler, love truly makes the world go 'round. . . . Amorous Taurus is ready for romance at any time of year, but it's easiest to find a new love in summer, when planets parade through Virgo, your love sign."[123] Then there are the daily newspapers with their astrological columns and the numerous almanacs and books devoted to the subject that fill the bookshelves of the big national bookstore chains.

Astrology got a big boost when it was revealed that U.S. President Ronald Reagan's wife, Nancy, paid astrologer Joan Quigley "$3,000 to $5,000 per month for her services." Nancy Reagan's reliance on astrology came to public notice in 1988 when President Reagan's chief of staff Donald Regan revealed in his book *For the Record* "that astrology exercised an inordinately powerful influence in the Reagan White House." Nancy Reagan's astrologer followed with her own book, *"What Does Joan Say? My Seven Years as White House Astrologer to Nancy and Ronald Reagan,* debuting with a first printing of 175,000 copies. In this book Quigley documents her consultations with Nancy Reagan."[124]

The Internet, with its vast, limitless ocean of cyberspace, has astrologers by the hundreds waiting for your call. "But, as a serious and systematic world view claiming the allegiance of many of the best intellects in every rank of society, astrology is dead. If it were asked what dethroned astrology, the answer lies in the general progress of science and scholarship. Astrology had been born in a geocentric world, and the Copernican revolution dealt it a shattering blow. The predictions of the astrologers do not survive the test of the experimental method."[125]

Stoics and Epicureans

What is the principle thing? To be able to endure adversity with a joyful heart; to bear
whatever betide just as if it were the very thing
you desired to have happen to you. For you
would have felt it your duty to desire it, had
you known that all things happen by divine de-
cree. Tears, complaints, lamentations are a rebellion [against divine order].

— the Stoic Seneca[126]

We have been born once and cannot be born a
second time; for all eternity we shall no longer
exist. But you, although you are not in control
of tomorrow, are postponing your happiness.
Life is wasted by delaying, and each one of us
dies without enjoying leisure.

— Epicurus[127]

In their attempts to find meaning in their lives and
develop a degree of self-sufficiency, many Romans, especially in the patrician class, adopted one of two op-
posing philosophies: Epicureanism or Stoicism.
Atheistic Epicureans believed in a universe formed by
cosmic chance and without order, thus leaving man free
to guide his own destiny. Pleasure is the ultimate good
and is, therefore, the principle goal in life. The two main
impediments to a life of happiness are fear of God and
fear of an afterlife. As Charles Norris Cochrane noted,
this completely materialistic philosophy "set up a moral
atomism which imposed no effective check upon the

sway of individual caprice and provided no basis for political and social cohesion."[128]

For the strong, serious-minded, stolid characters, there were the Stoics, founded by the Greek philosopher Zeno around 300 B.C. Unlike the Epicureans, the Stoics taught that man lived in an ordered rational world and that virtue was the greatest good and could only be gained by living according to pure reason. The path to true freedom lay in doing one's duty and shunning passion, injustice, and self-indulgence. The four cardinal virtues were wisdom, courage, justice, and temperance. For many of the serious, sober-minded Romans, the stern ethics of the Stoics was appealing. Thus, prior to the rise of Christianity, Stoicism rather than Epicureanism was the most influential philosophy in the Roman Empire.

Stoicism was "one of the last, if not one of the greatest, attempts of classical *scientia* to meet the legitimate demand of thinking men for a just and reasonable world; and, in this sense, it claimed the merit of a system which was 'reverent without superstition.'"[129] However, for the common Roman citizen, the cerebral, astringent ethics of stoic philosophy with its iron-bound fatalism, held little attraction. They were looking for a religious experience that was immediate, warm, emotive, and with the promise of an afterlife.

The Mystery Religions

Everywhere they (Romans) entertain the gods and adopt them as their own; they raise altars even to the unknown deities, and to the spirits of the dead. Thus is it that they adopt the sacred rites of all nations.

— Minucius Felix Octavius[130]

While the gods and goddesses of old Rome served as patriotic symbols and totems, their empty, legalistic formalism could not fill the aching spiritual vacuum of her citizens. The intrinsic, irresistible fatalism in astrology with its iron-clad determinism also could not satisfy the souls of a people longing for an intense religious experience with a promise of an afterlife. They turned in large numbers to numerous saviors with promises of eternal bliss. "The pagan savior cults responded with their thrilling, dramatic, sometimes orgiastic ceremonials, their solemn rituals of progressive initiation (mysterion), and their holy books claiming unique revelation and knowledge. The strength of these religions was that they were all things to all people; and they were among the most vigorously lively features of contemporary Roman society and thought."[131] These mystery cults were to provide a way station in the spiritual journey of the Roman people from the gods of their ancestors to Christianity.

Of the Eastern mystery cults, those of Cybele, Isis, and Mithras were the most popular. From Syria came Cybele, the Great Mother, who was originally worshipped with orgiastic dancing the Roman authorities eventually prohibited. Later, they eased their restrictions and the cult of Cybele once again flourished. However, Isis (Egypt's contribution to the Roman pantheon), the gentler goddess of goodness and consolation, was by far the more popular, being enthusiastically embraced by the Roman populace. Women were especially attracted to the elaborate and mystical initiation rites. After a 10-day initiation procedure, the devotees were treated to an all-night drama depicting the death and resurrection of Isis' husband, Osiris. His miraculous resurrection, "supposedly achieved by Isis herself, through the depth and poignancy of her grief, was the central emotional appeal of Isis' cult. In reconstructing the event, her followers believed that they too were being reborn and, in fact, gained immortality."[132]

From Persia came Mithras, representing war, justice, contract, light, and faith. Being popular with the Roman army, the cult spread rapidly throughout the Roman Empire. Mithraism was one of the last Eastern mystery cults to reach the West. It was also "one of the most vigorous, and in the final death struggle of paganism it emerged as a chief rival and opponent of Christianity."[133] Mithras is usually shown as a young god in the act of slaying a sacrificial bull. Mithra offered his devotees the figure of a heroic leader who would defend and help his followers in their struggle against evil, with eternal bliss as their reward. As the eminent French historian H. Daniel-Rops comments:

> There was a fundamental affinity between the military mind and the spirit of this religion which presented life as a heroic battle against the forces of evil, and which called certain of its superior initiates "soldiers." Mithras the chaste, virile hero, who despised the feminine softness

in which so many of the Asian gods delighted, offered an ideal of fervour and heroism, a kind of Nietzschean conception of the world. In a sick society, this vigorous doctrine was like a call to youth and sanity. Its success was extraordinary.[134]

Mithraism was a masculine religion that emphasized valor and heroic effort at the expense of mercy and love. As Daniel-Rops observed, "It was a religion of the will, not of the heart."[135]

Observations

Today, mounting evidence that society is out of control breeds disillusionment with science. In consequence, we witness a garish revival of mysticism. Suddenly, astrology is the rage. Zen, yoga, seances, and witchcraft become popular pastimes. Cults form around the search for Dionysian experience, for non-verbal and supposedly non-linear communication. We are told it is more important to "feel" than to "think."

— Alvin Toffler[136]

There is a great deal of similarity between our post-industrial society and pre-Christian Rome. The social pathologies resulting from a multicultural society, with its attendant social stresses and strains, with the loss of faith in the established religious institutions, and the flight into the Romantic and irrational are all too familiar. As with ancient Rome, we are also witnessing the enthusiastic assimilation of exotic Eastern mysticism. However, unlike the Romans, we have an added anxiety known as "Future Shock . . . the dizzying disorientation brought on by the premature arrival of the future."[137] Another difference—and I might add more sinister one—is that while the Roman mystery cults provided a way station in the spiritual journey of the Roman people from the gods of their ancestors to Christianity, the New Age movement has turned its back on Christ and His Gospel. This is a phenomenon I explored at some length in my book *The Pearl*, when I wrote that "it is crucial to understand that the paganism of classical antiquity that society came out of into Christianity is substantially different from the new paganism that society is sliding into from Christianity."[138]

However, the New Age movement, with its self-centered focus, "will not prevail" says John Stockhouse, professor of theology and culture at Regent College in Vancouver, British Columbia. "Christianity spoke with authority on matters that the (Roman) mystery cults never addressed. It's the same today. No other religion, then or now, possesses the same clarity of moral vision or offers a hope of eternal life based on an actual resurrection."[139]

CHAPTER FOUR

The Sorcerer's Apprentice: Madame Blavatsky

Do not pay attention to dreams or soothsayers, but be guided by trust in the all-powerful grace of Jesus Christ.

— Elder Moses of Optima[140]

No book on the New Age movement would be complete without reference to Helena Petrovna Blavatsky (1831–1891), whose teachings in the occult have exercised enormous influence with the contemporary New Age movement. Together with the American Colonel Henry Steel Olcott, she founded the Theosophical Society in New York in 1875 — an international group of occultists who claimed that reincarnation was the path to a purified humanity — "they sponsored the first cremation in America."[141] Through their society, they introduced the West to the religions of the East, including the ideas of reincarnation, karma, and astral projection. These nineteenth century occult trailblazers sowed the seeds for the later flowering of the modern New Age movement. However, the undisputed leader and guiding spirit was the brilliant, powerful, magnetic Madame Blavatsky. She claimed to have a communion with disembodied eastern spirit masters who revealed to her, and her alone, the secrets of the cosmos. British author Peter Washington provides a colorful description of her in early middle age:

> Her physical presence was hard to forget. Though not approaching the seventeen and a half stone (245 lbs.) she later achieved by eating fatty foods, including her favourite fried eggs floating in butter, she was already stout. She had light brown hair 'crinkled like a negro or a cotswold ewe' and magnetic eyes, variously described as blue, grey-blue and azure. High cheekbones and a broad massive face with a flattened nose completed the exotic appearance suggested by shabby fantastic clothes. . . . In later life she developed a taste for loose, badly fitting robes, preferring a sort of red flannel dressing-gown. She smoked incessantly, she carried the materials (she rolled her own) for her cigarettes in a furry pouch made out of an animal head worn round her neck. Her hands were usually covered with rings, some with genuine stones, and she looked like a badly wrapped and glittering parcel. She talked incessantly in a guttural voice, sometimes wittily and sometimes crudely . . . fonder of animals than of people; unsnobbish, unpretentious, scandalous, capricious, and rather noisy. She was also humorous, vulgar, impulsive and warm-hearted, and she didn't give a hoot for anyone or anything. . . . In her most typical photographs she looks straight out of the picture with the air of a woman used to confront-

ing difficulties and getting her own way. Yet there is a hint of melancholy in the heavy features. This is a pugnacious face which has been through a great deal.[142]

While the stated objectives of the Theosophical Society was to promote the universal brotherhood of man, the essential oneness of all religions, and the research of psychic phenomena, the Society in reality proved to be the platform whereby Madame Blavatsky could perform her occult powers. Despite being repeatedly exposed as a fraud, this forceful personality was still able to attract a large following, including luminaries such as the playwright George Bernard Shaw and the poet William Butler Yeats.

Bad Omens

In August 1831, in the Ukrainian town of Ekaterinoslav (Glory of Catherine), named after Catherine the Great, a hasty baptism had been arranged. For Helena Petrovna von Hahn had been born prematurely and in delicate health, at the height of a vicious Asiatic cholera plague that was sweeping Russia. The local peasants thought that it was a bad omen to be born at such a time. The baptismal ceremony took place in a large room in the mansion of her grandparents. Due to a number of plague deaths in the household, coffins were piled high in other rooms, awaiting burial. Relatives describe the dramatic scene that follows.

The large room was filled to capacity on that hot August day, with relatives and friends holding lighted candles, eager to witness the baptismal ceremony. In the center of the room with their splendid gold robes and long hair stood the Orthodox priest and his three assistants, one of whom was gently swinging a censor that filled the great room with blue clouds of fragrant incense. Surrounding them were three pairs of godparents, as well as three pairs of sponsors and household serfs. Standing immediately behind the priest was the baby's child-aunt, Princess Helena Pavlovna Dolgorukova's three-year-old daughter, Nadyezhda. Possibly overcome by the heat, and tired of standing, she sat down on the floor with her candle unnoticed by the adults. During the ceremony, when the sponsors were in the act of renouncing Satan by spitting three times, the child's lighted candle caught the robes of the priest. No one noticed until it was too late. The old priest and several bystanders suffered burns.[143]

This was one more bad omen that had surrounded the birth of Helena Petrovna. According to the superstitious beliefs of czarist Russia, "she was doomed from that day forward to a life of trouble and vicissitude."

CHAPTER FOUR

Priestess of Isis

As a child, Helena Petrovna's behavior was considered unmanageable, she "never hesitated to throw a temper tantrum when she could not get her way. The slightest contradiction," recalled her Aunt Nadyezhda, "brought on an outburst of passion, often a fit of convulsions."[144] She was also plagued with visions and voices—invisible playmates, one of whom was a hunchbacked little boy. Her relatives frequently found her earnestly conversing with invisible spirits. Her family certainly looked upon Helena Petrovna as a queer, extraordinary child as her sister Vera records in her book *Juvenile Reflections Compiled for My Children*. Helena "was the strangest girl one has ever seen," even to the point of calling her "crazy Helen." Later, she began to experience terrifying hallucinations in which she was pursued by the "terrible glaring eyes" of inanimate objects.

> She would shut her eyes tight during such visions and run away to hide from the ghostly glances . . . screaming desperately and frightening the whole household. At other times, she would be seized with fits of laughter, explaining them as the amusing pranks of her invisible companions.[145]

When reading of Helena Blavatsky's early life, I am reminded of John Warwick Montgomery's observation: "The transition from a 'sixth sense' to the presence of angelic or demonic forces is a short step, and most mediums and spiritualists easily take it."[146] Her abilities as a medium soon began to show when she began to take dictation from an old deceased German woman who dictated to Helena her life's story. Helena was able to write reams of manuscripts in "clear, old fashioned, peculiar handwriting and grammar in German" — a language she had never learned to write or even speak well. Her worried parents summoned a priest, who sprinkled holy water during the sessions, declaring it to be the work of the devil. However, through Helena, the disembodied spirit blunted the priest's objections by declaring that she was in the presence of God, the Virgin Mary, and the angelic host. The sessions continued.[147]

According to her friend and biographer Alfred Percy Sinnett, Helena "from her earliest recollections... would sometimes have visions of a mature protector, whose imposing appearance dominated her imagination from a very early period. This protector was always the same, his features never changed; in [later] life she met him as a living man, and knew him as though she had been brought up in his presence."[148]

In 1848, at the age of seventeen, she married Nikifor Blavatsky, a man in his early forties and Vice-Governor of Yerevan in the Caucasusords. As the priest recited the words to her, "Thou shalt honor and obey thy husband," at the hated word *shalt*, "her face was seen to flush angrily, then to become deadly pale. She was overheard to mutter in response through her set teeth — 'Surely I *shall not*.'"[149] The marriage was a complete failure, with Helena fleeing her husband and Russia three months after the wedding. She arrived in the

United States twenty-five years later, describing the intervening years as a "veiled" time. What little she did reveal of these "veiled" twenty-five years displays a romantic imagination that requires a high degree of credulity to be entirely believed. She listed her various occupations as a circus bareback rider, a concert pianist in Serbia, an importer of ostrich feathers in Paris, operating an ink factory in Odessa, and an interior decorator to the Empress Eugenie. She claimed to have traveled disguised as a man and to have fought as a soldier in the army of Giuseppe Garibaldi at the battle of Mentana (1867), where she "had been wounded five times. Her left arm was broken in two places by a saber stroke, she had a musket bullet embedded in her right shoulder and another in her leg. Finally, she had been left for dead in a ditch."[150] She claimed that she evaded death again when a Greek ship, the *Eumonia*, blew up with great loss of life. As author Peter Washington comments, "Blavatsky talked brilliantly and indiscreetly about herself, but rarely said exactly the same thing twice."[151]

One of Blavatsky's boasts was her seven-year sojourn in Tibet. "The significance of this claim rests on the traditional belief that seven years is the period of apprenticeship for candidates seeking initiation into esoteric mysteries. Blavatsky became a celebrity by claiming that, not only had she been "chosen" to reach the highest level of initiation in the occult hierarchy permitted to human beings, but that she owed her advancement to certain "Himalayan Masters" with whom she had studied in their mountain homes."[152] However, outside of her word, there is no evidence that she ever entered closed, inhospitable Tibet.[153] Besides, as author Peter Washington writes, "the strongest argument against the idea is a practical one: the thought of the breathless, tactless, and massively stout Blavatsky managing to climb steep mountains in brutal weather while concealing herself from trained observers is just too difficult to imagine."[154]

Blavatsky claimed to be guided by ascended (through previous reincarnations) spiritual masters possessing extraordinary psychic powers who had "astral" bodies and could materialize or dematerialize at will. Known as the Great White Brotherhood of Masters or Mahatmas, while dwelling mainly in Egypt, Tibet, and the Himalayas, they traveled around the universe working wonders communicating with each other through a form of mental telepathy. This Brotherhood only revealed themselves to a select few. In 1877, Blavatsky published her first great work on occult knowledge, *Isis Unveiled,* most of which she claimed was dictated to her by the Brotherhood while in a trancelike state. "At other times, a master would take over her body and write for her, unquestionably a help with a book running to half a million words."[155]

Blavatsky was a true Romantic in her fixation with the supernatural and the paranormal. She died in London in 1891, repeatedly exposed during her lifetime as a fraud and denounced and disowned by her business partner, Colonel Olcott.

Spiritualism—A Nineteenth Century Parlor Game

What would I have said six years ago to any-body who predicted that before the enlightened nineteenth century was ended, hundreds of thousands of people in this country would be-lieve themselves able to communicate with the ghosts of their grandfathers!

—George Templeton Strong, 1855[156]

The latter half of the nineteenth century was a great age of spiritualism in both Europe and North America. Charles Darwin's theory of evolution in his monumen-tal work *Origin of Species*, the growing prestige of sci-ence, and the new biblical exegesis that attempted to drain the miraculous from Scripture and humanize Christ all took their toll. Many people, like their eight-eenth century counterparts, could not endure the arid spiritual environment. As we discussed in the previous chapter, this condition leads to anxiety, uncertainty, in-security, and demoralization. On this point Cambridge scholar James Webb comments:

In circumstances of anxiety and uncertainty, superstition is likely to make a prominent showing. This is seen as perhaps a regression to infantile attitudes, or to beliefs acquired early in life and afterwards suppressed; or perhaps as a means of obtaining some sort of illusory con-trol over a frightening situation. During the nineteenth century crises of consciousness, this sort of situation was the order of the day; and superstition flourished. The most interesting facet of the flight from reason is the revival of the occult. Under this widely misunderstood heading are grouped an astonishing collection of subjects: hypnotism, magic, astrology, water-divining, 'secret' societies, and a multitude of similar topics of doubtful intellectual respectability.[157]

The fabric of mid-nineteenth century American life, writes Professor Bret E. Carroll,

seemed to be unraveling, stretched and torn by forces which promoted selfishness, materialism, fragmentation, and atomization as Americans drifted away from the past and toward modernity. Industrialization, urbanization, and the growth of commercial capitalism were rapidly altering the nation by the 1830s, and growing immigration added to the social flux by the late 1840s. The growth of population, the development of a mass society and culture, and the reality of cultural, ethnic, and religious pluralism encouraged among many middle-class Protestants a sense that social order was threatened and that their control over it was lost. . . . These unsettling developments combined to produce spiritual malaise, discomfort. . . . Most of those attracted to spiritualism found their deities distant, their cultural and social surroundings dis-

turbing, and their ministers and churches inef-
fectual in addressing the resulting uneasi-
ness.[158]

The emergence of nineteenth century spiritualism
occurred at a small wooden cottage at Hydesville,
Acadia, in New York State known as the "burned-over"
district. This term referred to that area of western New
York State "burned over" and exhausted by successive
waves of preachers fanning the flames of revival. In
March 1848, the Fox family was disturbed by strange
rappings that shook tables and chairs. The youngest
daughter of the household, Kate, asked the spirit to rap
out the number of times she flipped her fingers. After
establishing communication, a code was worked out,
whereby the spirit was able to identify himself as a man
who had been murdered in the house. An ardent contemporary spiritualist wrote of this event in a lofty,
gothic, Romantic style:

> The humble frame dwelling at Hydesville
> looms up into the proportions of a gigantic
> temple whose foundations are laid in the four
> corners of the earth, and the rough and rugged
> path which the bleeding feet of the Hydesville
> mediums seemed doomed to has now loomed
> out into the splendid proportions of the bridge
> which arches over the awful chasm of the
> grave, affording a transit for millions of aspir-
> ing souls into the glorious realities of eter-
> nity.[159]

Kate Fox and her older sister became much-sought-after mediums in the United States and England. The rise of this new cult was meteoric (e.g., by 1851 an estimated 100 mediums were operating in New York City alone).[160] Attempting to communicate with the dead by table rapping quickly became a popular pastime in Victorian drawing rooms on both sides of the Atlantic.

The movement was fueled not only by curiosity and fascination for the supernatural, but also for many people it offered convincing evidence of life after death. For the materialistic members of Victorian society who had lost their Christian faith, here was the promise of an afterlife based on observable data available to anyone. The possibility of communicating with the dead was especially attractive to those suffering the loss of loved ones. Even the exposure of the Fox sisters as frauds in 1881 (they admitted to producing the noise of the rappings by cracking their joints),[161] the cult did not suffer in popularity. In fact, this popularity carried over into the twentieth century. Field Marshal Sir Douglas Haig, Commander in Chief of the British forces in France during the First World War "seemed to move through the horrors of the First World War as if guided by some inner voice, speaking of a higher purpose and personal destiny. That, we now know, was not just appearance. Haig was a devotee both of spiritualistic practices and of fundamentalist religion. As a young officer he had taken to attending seances, where a medium put him in touch with Napoleon."[162]

Sir Arthur Conan Doyle (a lapsed Roman Catholic), the author of the famous Sherlock Holmes detective mysteries, had a lifelong interest in spiritualism and the occult. Upon the death of his son during the First World War in 1916, Conan Doyle declared himself a spiritualist and spent the remainder of his life propagating his faith. During the First World War, Britain and her Empire lost a million men. In Britain, the mortality for young men rose 800 percent between the years 1914–1918—a figure that cruelly transcended the boundaries of what could be emotionally borne.

To a grieving population, mediums held out the promise of establishing contact with lost sons, husbands, and sweethearts. In their grief and misery, many took this path, and Sir Arthur Conan Doyle was no exception: "'It was only in the time of war when all these splendid young fellows were disappearing from view,' he says, that he became completely convinced that spiritualism was all-important. He added that he has received so many letters from people who have been consoled by spiritualism that he could fill a room in his house with them."[163] During a number of seances with various mediums, Conan Doyle claimed to have established contact with his deceased son.

It was with a degree of shock, following his death in 1950, that Canadians learned that their famous wartime Prime Minister, William Lyon Mackenzie King, had been deeply dependent on mediums and spiritualism. A lifelong bachelor, Mackenzie King had a deep attachment to his mother, whose death in 1917 caused him great distress. However, after numerous seances, he was able to write:

My mother is nearer to me today than she was in her last day upon earth and I am nearer to her. . . . She has come back to me, and I have now the assurance that she is at my side and that we will be together for ever.[164]

Mackenzie King constantly resorted to mediums for guidance. In 1935, he asked ex-Prime Minister Sir Wilfred Laurier (1841–1919) "to advise him on how long to speak on the Address in reply to the Speech from the Throne; and Sir Wilfred said, 'Speak for an hour and a half. . . . Speak on trade and labour. . . . Try to touch the high spots only, give up reading figures, or quotations. Try to be humorous, light touches help to relieve the monotony.'"[166] During the war, in 1941, Sir Wilfred advises him to cross the Atlantic to England in a bomber plane but warns that the weather in September will not be good for flying. "During the 90's, Hillary Rodham Clinton, wife of U.S. President Bill Clinton, spoke of consulting the dead spirit of former First Lady Eleanor Roosevelt."[167]

Observations

If the sheer volume of New Age literature is any indication, channeling is possibly the single most important and definitive aspect of the New Age. It is certainly the activity which has had the greatest success in mobilizing support for the movement as a whole.[168]

Nor charmer, nor any one that consulteth pythonic spirits, or fortune telling, or that seeketh

the truth from the dead. For the Lord abhor-
reth all these things, and for these abominations
he will destroy them at thy coming.

—Deuteronomy 18:11–12

Belief in a soul is like the incest taboo, a universally
held belief in human culture: human beings have an
acute awareness of their own inner selves, including
thoughts, desires, and feelings. This is characterized by
a reflexive inwardness that is self-conscious rather than
mere consciousness—the ability to reflect on one's
thoughts and actions as we encounter other human beings. As with most human societies, the Church has always insisted, in keeping with the teaching of Christ,
that the soul is the immortal part of a human being. It is
for this reason that biblical injunctions against occult
practices such as necromancy (communicating with the
dead) exist because there is recognition of a deadly
spiritual reality. Not all spiritualistic phenomenon involving mediums can be dismissed as trickery, as the
Encyclopaedia Britannica is reduced to admitting: "It is
generally agreed that, when fraud is eliminated, there
remains a considerable residuum of phenomena osten-
sibly spiritualistic, whatever may be their explana-
tion."[169]

In keeping with the biblical prohibition, the Church
has always forbidden occult practices in any form because it leads the soul to a dependence on evil spirits
who, while claiming prophecy and superior wisdom,
lead the unwitting practitioners away from their Creator. Mediums, as we have seen in previous chapters,

destroy a person's moral compass by denying the reality of good and evil (e.g., "You must not resist what you call evil" — the spirit "John" speaking through medium Kevin Ryerson in *Dancing in the Light*[170]). Once this is accomplished, it is easy to convince people that they can create their own reality. In their denial of good and evil, New Agers live in a spiritual vacuum, free from ethics and that inhibiting conscience that Hamlet reminds us, "doth make cowards of us all."[171] Such a view creates a blindness to the suffering of others, as Professor Michael F. Brown observes:

> A moral framework in which people are thought capable of creating their own reality and the existence of evil is routinely called into question provides two logical avenues for the interpretation of illness, poverty, and other forms of suffering. The first is that they occur because the victims cannot or will not envision the world in ways that protect them from misfortune. Calamity originates in a failure of individual attitude or thought. A newsletter distributed by a channel in upstate New York, for example, asserted that the national problem of homelessness is nothing but an illusion, "the last out-picturing of a form of mental and emotional poverty." Poverty exists, in other words, because poor people think impoverished thoughts. Belief in the ability of the mind to pluck hardship from a loving universe can be traced to the New Thought movement of the nineteenth century. Mary Baker Eddy, the

founder of Christian Science, saw illness in these terms, and some of her contemporaries extended this line of thinking to account for poverty and its opposite. The alternative is that victims of illness or misadventures have chosen their own fate, usually at a "deep soul level" beneath everyday awareness. The logic here is that reincarnating selves need a range of learning experience in order to achieve spiritual maturity. The underlying eternal core of the self thus chooses certain challenges as part of the growth process.[172]

We see this mentality reflected in Shirley MacLaine's wondering about the death of her daughter's acting teacher who suffered a head-on collision and was burnt beyond recognition as to "why anyone would choose a death like that."

Many people grieving for loved ones approach mediums with the best of intentions. However, this can lead to great spiritual danger, as a dependence on mediums or channeling with their general anti-Christian bias can turn into pride and rebellion against God. For, ultimately, the continued attempt to contact deceased loved ones demonstrates a refusal to accept God's providence in our lives. We see this in the case of Mackenzie King, where his frequent use of mediums fed his need for empowerment and so drew him deeper. In her study of Mackenzie King, author Joy E. Esberey writes:

This progression was reinforced by his inability to submit totally to authority, to let God's will take its course; thus King failed to find the release and the sense of power and purpose in religion that others did. Instead, he was driven to more and more restless searching for the certainty which would allow him complete control over his destiny.[173]

The world of the occult exerts enormous power over its followers, as Helena Blavatsky, the archpriestess of the modern New Age movement, revealed to Vsevolod Soloviev, an old Russian friend. They met in Paris in 1884 when she was 53 and well steeped in the occult. In baring her soul to her old friend, this pathetic woman admitted to an almost Faustian bargain she felt incapable of breaking:

> I would gladly return, I would gladly be Russian, Christian, Orthodox. I yearn for it. But there is no returning; I am in chains; I am not my own.[174]

CHAPTER FIVE

The New Age Jesus

Jesus saith to them: But whom do you say that I am?

— Matthew 16:15

While the New Age movement places Christ on a very high pedestal in its pantheon of Ascended Masters, Enlightened Teachers, Gurus, etc., their view of Christ differs substantially from traditional Christianity. Even though they do not possess a single uniform view, however, most New Age views of Christ do betray an inherent Gnosticism.

Gnosticism

The question must be asked whether, behind the renewed interest in Gnosis, there is not something other than merely a taste for the exotic or the volatile search for the esoteric, whether there is not hidden the intuition of a secret affinity between our age of crises, riddled with anxiety and at the same time avid for change and thirsting for novelty, and the historical period between the second and third centuries A.D., when ancient Gnosticism established itself as a religious response to the acute problems of an "age of anxiety."[175]

Gnosticism is derived from the Greek word *gnostikos* – one who has *gnosis,* "knowledge." Gnosticism was a religious movement of late antiquity the Christian church came into contact with, encompassing various pantheistic sects who claimed to know the mysteries of the universe. They were dualists, believing that God created the spiritual world while the Devil created the earth and all matter. Therefore, since the world is produced from evil matter, it is alien to God. Some scholars have suggested that Augustine's views that sexual intimacy between husband and wife should only be for the procreation of children, which dominated the Western Church until the late nineteenth century, are Gnostic in origin.

As with New Agers, the inherent belief in salvation by knowledge or "revealed wisdom" rather than faith lies at the very core of Gnostic religion. Their *gnosis* lay beyond the forces of reason (i.e., not based on philosophical or intellectual deliberation, but on a perceived, mystical knowledge of nature and man). Like their present-day counterparts, they prided themselves in possessing a deep, mystical, cosmic wisdom.

In his work *A History of Philosophy,* Frederick Copleston had this to say about Gnosticism:

> To us today it is difficult to understand how Gnosticism could ever have been a danger to the Church or an attraction to a sane mind; but we have to remember that it arose at a time when a welter of philosophical schools and mystery-religions was seeking to cater for the spiritual needs of men. Moreover, esoteric and

theosophical systems, surrounded with the pseudo-glamour of 'eastern wisdom' have not entirely lost their attraction for some minds even in much more recent times.[176]

The Gnostic Christ by Adoption

Examine yourself that you may understand who you are, in what way you exist, and how you will come to be. . . . For he who has not known himself has known nothing. But he who has known himself has . . . already achieved knowledge about the Depth of the All.

> —the resurrected Christ to Judas Thomas from the Gnostic *Book of Thomas the Contender*[177]

Adoptionism was an early Christological heresy that taught Christ was merely a man who was only adopted by God at his baptism, where he received his divine power, rather than being seen as the pre-existent Son of God. Thus, here we have the Gnostic, Cosmic Christ of the New Age, who with his occultic wisdom will enlighten us and lead us to the self-realization of our own divinity. Therefore, the misfortunes that befall humanity are not offenses against a just and holy God, "but ignorance of human origins and human potential."[178]

In denying the divinity of Christ and looking upon Him as merely a man, a revealer of wisdom, the Gnostic view obviously collided with that of the Gospels. There-fore, relying on the Gospels for their source, they wrote their own twisted version. In their Apocalypse of Peter, we see their duality of spirit (good) and body (evil) ap-plied to the crucifixion, where Christ the spirit sits on the branch of a tree, watching and laughing at the bod-ily Christ being crucified:

> He whom you saw on the tree, glad and laughing, this is the living Jesus. But the one in whose hands and feet they drive nails is the fleshly part which is the substitute being put to shame, the one who came into being in his like-ness. . . . Be strong, for you are the one to whom these mysteries have been given, to know them through revelation that he whom they crucified is the first-born, and the home of demons, and the stony vessel in which they dwell, of Elohim, of the cross which is under the Law. But he who stands near him is the living Savior.[179]

Reincarnation

And as it has been appointed unto men once to die, and after this the judgment.

—Hebrews 9:27

To undermine a Christian's faith in the biblical Christ and transfer his allegiance to a New Age, non-judgmental, human Christ drained of His divinity, three basic stratagems are used:

(1) Discover hidden writings that contain long-lost truths of the cosmic Christ.

(2) Transfer primary allegiance from scriptural revelation to new revelations received through channelers and psychics.

(3) Develop an esoteric system of interpreting the Bible (a system that seeks hidden, inner meanings), so Jesus can be made to appear a New Age evangelist.[180]

In her book *Out on a Limb*, Shirley MacLaine describes a conversation she had (where all three stratagems are used) with David Manning, her psychic friend who led her into the world of the occult:

"You know that nothing is recorded in the Bible about Christ from the time he was about twelve until he began to really teach about thirty years old. Right?"

"Yes," Shirley answered, "I had heard about that and I just figured he didn't have much to say until he got older."

"Well, no," David responded, "a lot of people think that those eighteen missing years were spent travelling in and around India and Tibet and Persia and the Near East. There are all kinds of legends and stories about a man who sounds just like Christ. His description is matched everywhere and he said he was the son of God and he corroborated the beliefs of the Hindus that reincarnation was, in fact, true. They say he became an adept yogi and mastered complete control over his body and the physical world around him. He evidently went around doing all those miracles that were recorded later in the Bible and tried to teach people that they could do the same things too if they got in touch with their spiritual selves and their own potential power."[181]

The conversation then turns to the husband-and-wife team of Janet and Richard Bock, who had written a book and produced a documentary film purporting to show that Christ had traveled in India. During the discussion, Shirley's friend David again mentions that Christ had learned the theory of reincarnation from Indian masters and had taught this upon his return to Israel. To which Shirley responded, "Why aren't these teachings recorded in the Bible?"

David responds by telling her that the Bible does *indeed* contain the theory of reincarnation, but the Fifth Ecumenical Council of the Church (553) voted to erase the correct interpretations. This was done, he assures her, in order "to solidify Church control. . . . When the Church destroyed those teachings, it screwed up mankind from then on."[182] Let us submit these New Age theories to close scrutiny. We will start with reincarnation.

Reincarnation, or metempsychosis, is a theory of the transmigration of souls, usually associated with the ancient Egyptians, who are said to have practiced embalming to prevent or delay reincarnation. It is also fundamental to most of the religions and philosophies of India. This is not the case with Christianity, however, which explicitly denies it, for the teaching on the finality of death and judgment is almost thematic in the New Testament.

The four Gospels abound with the message of repentance in this life, as there is no further chance after death. Christ's parable about Lazarus and the rich man is transparently clear. When the rich man begged Abraham for mercy, Abraham replied: "Son, remember that thou didst receive good things in thy lifetime, and likewise Lazarus evil things, but now he is comforted; and thou art tormented. And besides all this, between us and you, there is fixed a great chaos: so that they who would pass from thence to you, cannot, nor from thence come hither" (Luke 16:25–26).

St. Paul reminds us that judgment follows immediately after death: "But we are confident, and have a good will to be absent rather from the body, and to be present with the Lord. And therefore we labor, whether absent or present to please him. For all must be manifested before the judgment seat of Christ, that every one may receive the proper things of the body, according as he hath done, whether it be good or evil" (2 Cor. 5:9–10). We also read: "In the day of good things be not unmindful of evils: and in the day of evils be not mindful of good things: For it is easy before God in the day of death to reward every one according to his ways" (Eccles. 11:27–28). The endless cycle of reincarnations could not be more explicitly denied.

Shirley MacLaine's friend David Manning told her that while the Bible taught reincarnation, the Fifth Ecumenical Council voted to erase the correct interpretations. This is totally incorrect on two accounts. First, the canon of the New Testament was ratified at a series of synods at Hippo Regius in 393, and at Carthage in 397 and 419. Second, the council's condemnation had nothing to do with reincarnation but in the belief of the existence of the soul prior to conception, as espoused by Origen (c.185–254). Origen was one of the most influential theologians of the early Church; however, he was heavily influenced by Greek philosophers, especially Plato and his teaching on the preexistence of souls, and it was this that led him into heresy.

The chief accusations against Origen's teachings are the following:

> making the Son inferior to the Father, and so being precursor of Arianism; spiritualizing away the resurrection of the body; denying hell, a morally enervating universalism; speculating about preexistent souls and world cycles; dissolving redemptive history into timeless myth by using allegorical interpretation, thus turning Christianity into a kind of Gnosticism.[183]

Historian Leo Donald Davis records the Fifth Ecumenical Council's condemnation:

> Influenced by Hellenic thought, Origen taught that because the good God always needed objects toward whom He could exercise His goodness He created from all eternity, spiritual,

101

intellectual beings, all equal among themselves. These beings became diversified and fell into matter in varying degrees through the exercise of their free will. Thus spiritual beings fallen from their primal perfection became angels, demons, human beings, even heavenly bodies. Anathemas 2, 3, 4, and 5 condemn this view. Origen's cosmological views necessarily included an insistence on the preexistence of human souls; though fallen into matter from their primal state, they have existed as creatures from all eternity and will, if good, return to their primal state. Anathemas 1 and 15 condemn these opinions.[184]

One can readily see how far removed some of Origen's writings are from orthodox Christianity, and why the Council had to condemn them. However, in many ways Origen is a tragic figure, for "his sympathizers and friends knew that he desired nothing so much as to be a loyal member of the church"[185] and, "If orthodoxy were a matter of intention, no theologian could be more orthodox than Origen, none more devoted to the Christian faith."[186] There is no doubt that Origen did have a tendency to reinterpret apparently literal statements as spiritual symbols or allegories. However, it is nonsense to assert that the Council "voted to erase the [these] correct interpretations . . . to solidify Church control." Correct in whose eyes—twenty-first century New Agers with an anti-Christian bias? Certainly not in the eyes of the early Church Fathers, who in asserting the finality of final judgment, clearly rejected endless reincarnations (e.g., Ignatius of Antioch, Justin Martyr, Ire-naeus, Hippolytus, Augustine, Gregory of Nyssa, Basil the Great, etc.).

Jesus among the Brahmins of India

> You shall not go after the strange gods of all the nations, that are around about you: Because the Lord thy God is a jealous God in the midst of thee: lest at any time the wrath of the Lord thy God be kindled against thee, and take thee away from the face of the earth.
>
> —Deuteronomy 6:14–15

This novel story of Jesus' travels in India originated with Nicolas Notovitch, a Russian war correspondent who traveled through Tibet in 1887. According to Notovitch, Tibetan monks informed him that sacred scrolls existed at Himis, a Buddhist monastery, that recorded the life of a grand lama (great monk) named Issa (the Tibetan name for "Jesus"). Eventually Notovitch was allowed to see the scroll and have it translated. The scroll revealed that "Jesus had wandered to India and to Tibet as a young man before he began his work in Palestine."[187] The scroll records Jesus embarking on this improbable journey:

> When Issa had attained the age of thirteen years, the epoch when an Israelite should take a wife, the house where his parents earned their living . . . began to be a place of meeting for rich and noble people, desirous of having for a son-

103

in-law the young Issa, already famous for his edifying discourses in the name of the almighty. Then it was that Issa left the parental house in secret, departed from Jerusalem, and with the merchants set out towards (the province of) Sind, with the object of perfecting himself in the Divine Word and of studying the laws of the great Buddhas.[188]

The scroll then describes Issa studying at the feet of India's holy men and how the priests of Brahma "taught him to read and understand the Vedas [India's most sacred scriptures], to cure by aid of prayer, to teach, to explain the holy scriptures to the people, and to drive out evil spirits from the bodies of men, restoring unto them their sanity."[189] Copies of these scrolls were never brought to the West for examination or study, and a *Washington Times* article reports that the "records" have been destroyed.[190]

A number of scholars have completely exploded Notovitch's story of Jesus' sojourn in India. The first was Professor F. Max Mullerfesso, an oriental scholar from Oxford University, who in 1894 published his findings in *The Nineteenth Century*, an academic journal. Following close behind Muller was Professor J. Archibald Douglas of Government College in Agra, India. This man took the trouble to take a three-month leave of absence and journey to the Himis Monastery. He reported his work in the June 1895 edition of *The Nineteenth Century*, in which his interview with the chief lama of the monastery was recorded. He revealed that the chief lama had been in office for fifteen years, thereby encompassing Notovitch's alleged visit and knew nothing of him. On being questioned about the sacred scroll on the life of Issa, he replied: "There is no such book in the monastery, and during my term of office no *sahib* (European) has been allowed to copy or translate any of the manuscripts in the monastery."[191] The chief lama further commented that "I have never heard of (a manuscript) which mentions the name Issa, and it is my firm and honest belief that none such exists. I have inquired of our principal Lamas in other monasteries of Tibet, and they are not acquainted with any books or manuscripts which mention the name of Issa."[192] When Douglas read passages from Notovitch's book, the chief lama responded, "Lies, lies, lies, nothing but lies!"[193]

The written interview was witnessed by the chief lama, "Douglas, and the interpreter, and on June 3, 1895, was stamped with the official seal of the lama."[194] In his summation, Douglas wrote: "I have visited Himis and have endeavoured by patient and impartial inquiry to find out the truth respecting N. Notovitch's remarkable story, with the result that, while I have not found one single fact to support his statements, all the weight of evidence goes to disprove them beyond all shadow of doubt. It is certain that no such passages as N. Notovitch pretends to have translated exist in the monastery of Himis, and therefore it is impossible that he could have 'faithfully reproduced' the same."[195]

Other scholars have followed in exploding this myth; however, it continues to be a cherished belief of New Agers. For a more complete treatment of this subject, I would recommend *The Counterfeit Christ of the New Age Movement* by Ron Rhodes.

Observations

Jesus said to them: Amen, amen, I say unto you, before Abraham was made, I am.

—John 8:58

As we enter the twenty-first century, the enduring power and fascination of Jesus of Nazareth continues to capture the imagination and minds of people. His teaching inspired and permeated Europe, creating a brilliant Christian civilization whose global cultural contributions have been enormous. Today, the New Age movement likes to speak about the religion *of* Jesus in contrast to the religion *about* Jesus. The implication, of course, is that Jesus was a man among men, a great prophet with a heightened sense of the power and presence of God. It was the Church, of course, which created a religion about Jesus.

Jesus, however, did not give us the option of looking upon Him as a mere prophet or holy man. He unambiguously declared His divinity (Matt. 22:41–45; 26:61–64; John 10:30–33). In John 10:7–9, Jesus tells us that that no one can enter salvation except through Him. However, while at the dawn of creation "God created man in his own image and likeness" (Gen. 1:27), the New Age movement has created God in their own image and likeness. The divinization of man, by necessity, must result in the humanization of God. Man tells God "that as I increase you must decrease."

The offering of the serpent in the Garden of Eden always holds a strong allure by appealing to our pride, promising salvation by knowledge or "revealed wisdom" rather than by faith. With this promise comes the self-realization of our own divinity — becoming Godlike by knowing good from evil. The warning of Christ regarding the deceit and cunning of Satan echo down the centuries: "He was a murderer from the beginning, and he stood not in the truth; because truth is not in him. When he speaketh a lie, he speaketh his own: for he is a liar, and the father thereof. But if I say the truth, you believe me not" (John 8:44–45).

The New Age Movement Enters Mainline Christianity

> Jesus knew his worth, his success fed his self-esteem. . . . He suffered the cross to sanctify his self-esteem. And he bore the cross to sanctify your self-esteem. And *the cross will sanctify the ego trip*.
>
> —Pastor Robert Schuller[196]

> In the whole range of evil thoughts, none is richer in resources than self-esteem; for it is to be found almost everywhere, and like some cunning traitor in a city it opens the gates to all the demons.
>
> — *The Philokalia*[197]

In addition to influencing popular culture, business, and education, the New Age movement has also penetrated Christianity. Shirley MacLaine would certainly endorse Pastor Robert Schuller's advise: "You don't know what power you have within you! . . . You can make your world into anything you choose. Yes, you can make your world into whatever you want it to be."[198] This sort of crass advice becomes outrageous when delivered under Christian auspices. Tragically, this preacher wields enormous influence. In *Christianity Today*, we learn that "Schuller is now reaching more non-Christians than any other religious leader in North America."[199] It is very obvious that Pastor Schuller espouses a very different Christianity than that of the Gospels. In the following, he completely emasculates the central Gospel message—mankind's redemption from its sinful state:

> I don't think anything has been done in the name of Christ and under the banner of Christianity that has proven more destructive to human personality and, hence, counterproductive to evangelism enterprise than the often crude, uncouth, and unchristian strategy of attempting to make people aware of their lost and sinful condition.[200]

In opposition to this message, we find that "John was in the desert baptizing, and preaching the baptism of penance, unto the remission of sins" (Mark 1:4), and Christ told the Pharisees, "I came not to call the just, but sinners to repentance" (Luke 5:32).

In early 2000, over 1,300 people descended on Oregon State University for the Trinity Institute's national conference, "God at 2000." While the aim of the conference was to promote "theological renewal" for Episcopal Church clergy, "the cavalcade of liberal speakers envisioned a new religious world in which syncretistic consensus would replace Christian orthodoxy."[201] Conference speakers included South Africa's Anglican Archbishop Desmond Tutu, Marcus Borg of the Jesus Seminar, Harvard professor Diana Eck, Benedictine nun Joan Chittister, former nun Karen Armstrong, and

George Washington University's Islamic scholar Seyyed Hossein Nasr.

In his address to the conference, Episcopalian Marcus Borg supported "a brand of 'Pantheism' that rejects notions of a personal God in favor of a broader universal spirit."[202] In an apologetic tone, he informs the conference that:

> I grew up in a time and place where it was taken for granted that Christianity was the only true religion and Jesus the only way of salvation. That's why we had missionaries. . . . I find it literally incredible to think that the God of the whole universe has chosen to be known in only one religious tradition, which just fortunately happens to be my own.[203]

Former nun Karen Armstrong told the conference that she is "amazed by Buddha's insights," and that there is so much wisdom in all of them. In fact, Armstrong claims that she "cannot see any of them as better or superior. All of them have given me so much."[204] The other speakers spoke along similar lines, with one glaring exception, the Moslem Professor Seyyed Hossein Nasr. As Mark Tooley observed: "It was indeed paradoxical that a Christian-sponsored conference, intended for Christian clergy and featuring a majority of speakers who are affiliated with Christian churches, had to rely almost exclusively on an Islamic speaker to imply that there are still some theological and ethical absolutes. The speakers who professed to be Christians were, in contrast, nearly all eager to embrace a new global and relativistic spirituality that consigns traditional Christianity to irrelevance."

Professor Nasr, while agreeing that "every religion is a face that God has turned to a particular humanity," reminded the conference that God is "absolute" and warned them against "falling down and relativising everything." For "if you only accept that your religion is relative, you will not follow it. . . . There must be something of absoluteness within religion. . . . Otherwise, there will just be languages that don't mean anything." Perhaps this Islamic scholar had some of the conference speakers in mind when he referred to "languages that don't mean anything."[205]

However, in spite of Professor Nasr's sage, cautionary advice, Catholic nun and activist Joan Chittister summed up the attitude of her fellow liberal speakers: "Surely there is no one participating in this conference who really believes that this conference is about 'God at 2000.' This conference is about us at 2000."[206]

Pentecostal/Charismatics and the New Age Movement

The New Age movement's one-world vision is paralleled in the Pentecostal/charismatic movement's transcendence of conventional denominational, national, and ethnic boundaries. American Pentecostalism has gone expansionist. Pentecostal-style worshippers are now found within all 150 traditional non-Pentecostal ecclesiastical confessions and families, in 8,000 ethnolinguistic cultures, and in myriads of state-sponsored

churches worldwide. . . . Though many differences remain between specific groups within the movement as
a whole (as in the case in the New Age movement), the
emphasis in recent times has been on unity in the Holy
Spirit rather than on theological argumentation.[207]

American religious historian Catherine Albanese, in
her address to the American Society of Church History
(1988), identified striking parallels between the New
Age movement and Christian fundamentalism. The
parallels she identified "included each movement's focus on personal transformation, healing, direct spiritual
experience, the reality of continuing revelation, a pecu-
liarly American species of religious materialism, and a
democratized spirituality that 'fell forward' into visions
of the millenium."[208] Intrigued with Albanese's insights,
historian Phillip Lucas identified the Pentecostals and
the charismatics as most closely paralleling the New
Age movement.[209] "Pentecostals" are those who are in
Pentecostal denominations (e.g., Assemblies of God,
Foursquare Gospel, United Pentecostal Church, etc),
while "charismatics" refer to those who remain within
their own non-Pentecostal denominations (e.g., Roman
Catholics, Episcopalians, Lutherans, etc.). Both groups,
however, are united in their emphasis in baptism in the
Holy Spirit, evidenced by "speaking in tongues," and
exuberant, spontaneous, emotionally charged worship
with upraised hands. An evangelical missionary described United Pentecostal Church services as follows:

> United Pentecostals really seem to enjoy their
> meetings. The emotionally charged atmosphere
> of their church services offers a feeling of joy, of

fiesta, and of the sensational (miracles, tongues, healing) that thrills, excites, and lifts these humble believers from the dreariness and drudgery of daily life. . . . Then there is freedom in their meetings—liberty to pray aloud, to pray all at once, to stand and shout, and to interject an "amen," a "'hallelujah," "praise the Lord" as they wish. . . . This liberty is often mentioned by both pastors and members as a major factor in the appeal of their meetings.[210]

In addition to an ultraconservative Protestant theology, an intense millenarianism, and expectancy of the imminent Second Coming of Christ is usually present.

Lucas notes that the Pentecostal and charismatic movements has ballooned into "the largest Christian movement of the twentieth century."[211] In David Barrett's comprehensive 1988 study, there are over 176 million Pentecostals and 123 million Protestant and Catholic charismatics worldwide, with 22.5 million Pentecostals and 43.2 million charismatics in North America alone.[212] Pentecostal Christianity displays a strong doctrinal individualism and independence of local congregations that has resulted in numerous divisions. The dry, arid services of mainline Protestant churches and the post-Vatican II Mass, devoid of mystery and ritual drama, have drained religion of its non-rational quality—the emotional, mystical, and poetic—thus contributing to the incredible growth of the Pentecostal/charismatic movement.

From baptism in the Holy Spirit, the Pentecostal/charismatics believe that the gifts of speaking in tongues (glossolalia), the ability to interpret these tongues, the gift of prophecy, the power of healing, "to utter words of wisdom, to discern spirit entities and to exorcise demons" become a reality.[213] Lucas insists that Pentecostal/charismatics share parallels with New Agers in their search for sacred power and experience (e.g., "rediscovery of invisible realms of sacred power and each movement's emphasis on ecstatic, emotional experience of this power"). As Lucas points out:

> The New Age movement, too, is strongly oriented to experiential encounters with sacred power. . . . Many New Agers accept the existence of a universal energy that differs from more common forms of energy like heat and light. This universal power is believed to undergird and permeate all existence. It goes by many names, including prana, mana, odic force, orgone energy, and ch'i. The Pentecostal/charismatic movement's concept of the Holy Spirit is in some ways analogous to this. It is the divine force moving behind the miraculous events of healing, prophecy, glossolalia, and exorcism. It is the point where God's sacred power enters the human realm and manifests itself tangibly to human agents.[214]

Both Pentecostal/charismatics and New Agers believe they have access to immediate spiritual experience and power. For New Agers, this usually involves consulting a "channeler" or "medium." This is an individual who enters a trancelike state in order to allow dead humans, disembodied spirits, ascended masters, etc., to impart to us a superior wisdom. As I noted in Chapter 4, "If the sheer volume of New Age literature is any indication, channeling is possibly the single most important and definitive aspect of the New Age. It is certainly the activity which has had the greatest success in mobilizing support for the movement as a whole."[215] It is estimated that there are over one thousand channelers practicing their craft in the Los Angeles area.[216]

Lucas sees parallels between New Age channeling and the Pentecostal/charismatic phenomena of "speaking in tongues" and "prophecy." To support his position, Lucas quotes charismatic writer Don Basham, who describes speaking in tongues as "a form of prayer in which the Christian yields himself to the Holy Spirit and receives from the Spirit a supernatural language with which to praise God."[217] Since the language of "tongues" is completely unintelligible, a "Spirit-filled" second person with the gift to interpret is necessary to translate the message for the community. Lucas observes that "some commentators have remarked that these spiritual guidances or ecstatic utterances have similarities to those evidenced by shamans in traditional folk religions. What is clear is that for both New Agers and Pentecostalist/charismatics, these events are experienced as a dramatic breakthrough of sacred power into the ordinary world, as an intensely personal, often ecstatic interaction with this power, and as compelling evidence of the proximity of other realms of being."[218]

Lucas cites the focus of both New Agers and Pentecostal/charismatics on personal healing and transformation as being another parallel. This focus on personal transformation has its origins in the founders of the human potential movement and humanistic psychology, Abraham Maslow, Carl Rogers, and Rollo May. For most New Agers, personal transformation is the "Holy Grail" of their spiritual quest. The Esalen Institute at Big Sur, California, blending psychology with Eastern religion, proved to be a useful "laboratory where human potential theorists could test ideas and techniques."[219]

Personal healing and transformation is also a major goal within the Pentecostal/charismatic movement and is made achievable by undergoing the "second blessing" or "baptism of the Holy Spirit." Following this initiation, personal growth and realization of one's potential are pursued by large scale use of "New Age group dynamics, popular psychology, New Thought teachings, and meditation techniques" by both liberal and traditionalist followings within the Pentecostal/charismatic movement. Lucas cites charismatic leaders like Josephine Ford "recommending the development of democratic, Esalen-type group structures and processes for their prayer groups. Interpersonal honesty and non-verbal forms of communication such as handholding, embracing, and massage were encouraged."[220] In 1978, the well-known charismatic leader Ruth Carter-Stapleton started a retreat center outside Dallas, Texas, named "Holovita," where she offers "an eclectic mix of spiritual therapies including directed visualizations and meditation. (Visualization techniques are, of course, a common staple of New Age self-help therapy.)"[221]

By the mid-1980's, the New Age movement's concept of "positive thinking" and achieving "personal prosperity" had so permeated the Pentecostal/charismatic movement that its traditional leaders were openly deploring the rampant materialism of their flock. "People are so engaged in making money, subconsciously mammon has become their god until this has clouded, in many places, the real fervor, fire, and New Testament zeal that comes with Pentecostal experience."[222]

The heart of the "prosperity gospel" world is the Word-Faith movement, spearheaded by the multidenominational Trinity Broadcasting Network of Costa Mesa, California. This network beams Word-Faith preachers like Kenneth Hagin, Kenneth Copeland, Frederick Price, John Avanzini, Robert Tilton, Marilyn Hickey, Paul Yonggi Cho, Charles Capps, Jerry Savelle, Morris Cerullo, and Paul Crouch to millions of viewers worldwide. Trinity Broadcasting Network (TBN) is seen on over 1500 television stations, 16 satellites, the Internet, and thousands of cable systems around the world. They also produce more original Christian programs than any other religious network. This is a powerful voice where "just about every night on TBN a person can tune in and learn how to gain wealth by following the prosperity formulas of Word-Faith teachers. These formulas, however, have more in common with cultic metaphysics than with Christianity."[223] The "name it and claim it" gospel owes much to the meta-physical school of thought espoused by Phineas Quimby. Quimby's "New Thought" insists that, by using the power of positive affirmation, people can create their own reality. By employing the technique of "creative visualization," a person can supposedly transform mental images into tangible reality. Author Ron Rhodes goes on to explain that:

> According to New Thought, human beings can experience health, success, and abundant life by using their thoughts to define the condition of their lives. New Thought proponents subscribe to the "law of attraction." This law says that just as like attracts like, so our thoughts can attract the things they want or expect. Negative thoughts are believed to attract dismal circumstances; positive thoughts attract more desirable circumstances. Our thoughts can be either creative or destructive. New Thought sets out to teach people how to use their thoughts creatively.[224]

The following is a small sampling of the biblical insights these Word-Faith preachers of TBN offer their viewing audience. As perverse as they are—and they are perverse—they are also far enough "wacko" as to enter the realm of humor. Kenneth Hagin assures his viewers that God wishes His followers to be rich and successful: "He wants His children to eat the best, He wants them to wear the best clothing, He wants them to drive the best cars, He wants them to have the best of everything." Frederick Price could not agree more: "If the Mafia can drive around in Lincoln Continental town cars, why can't the King's Kids?"[225] For the more hesitant viewers, skeptical of this material cornucopia, Robert Tilton assures them that "not only is worrying a sin, but being poor is a sin when God promises prosperity."[226]

For those who fret about fashion and the expense of designer clothing, John Avanzini tells his viewers to relax:

> John 19 tells us that Jesus wore designer clothes. Well, what else you gonna call it? Designer clothes—that's blasphemy. No, that's what we call them today. I mean, you didn't get the stuff He wore off the rack. It wasn't a one-size-fits-all deal. No, this was custom stuff. It was the kind of a garment that kings and rich merchants wore. Kings and rich merchants wore that garment.[227]

Frederick Price gives us an insight as to how Jesus could afford designer clothing:

> The Bible says that He [Jesus] had a treasurer— a treasury (they called it "the bag"); that they had one man who was the treasurer, named Judas Iscariot; and the rascal was stealing out of the bag for three-and-a-half years, and nobody knew that he was stealing. You know why? Because there was so much in it. . . . Nobody could tell that anything was missing. . . . Besides that, if Jesus didn't have anything, what

do you need a treasury for? A treasury is for surplus, it's not for that which you're spending. It's only for surplus—to hold until you need to spend it. Therefore, He must have had a whole lot that needed to be held in advance that He wasn't spending. So He must have had more than He was living on.[228]

Comedian Ray Stevens sings a song entitled "Would Jesus Wear a Rolex?" on his CD *Crackin' Up* – a song that pillories the TV preachers and their wealth and prosperity gospel:

Would He wear a pinkie ring? / Would He drive a fancy car? / Would His wife wear furs and diamonds? / Would His dressing room have a star? / If He came back tomorrow, there's something I'd like to know, / Would Jesus wear a Rolex on His television show?

In 1987, the John Ankerberg television show devoted a special 6-part series revealing "the degree to which such New Age practices as visualization, seeking advice from an inner guide, rebirthing, and listening to relaxation tapes have permeated the Pentecostal/charismatic movement."[229]

There is also within the Pentecostal/charismatic and New Age movements a shared anti-authoritarian bias. Both movements enjoy a decentralized structure, with most New Agers operating through a form of "networking," with decisions gained through consensus. However, ultimate authority lies within the individual, even when "gurus" or "masters" are involved, it is the New Ager who "decides which teachings or groups meet his needs based upon interior spiritual guidance."[230]

Bolstered by the doctrine of *sola scriptura* ("by Scripture alone"), the Pentecostal/charismatic authority also lies with the individual. For with the Holy Spirit guiding them in the correct interpretation of Scripture, they become their own supreme pontiff. With this personal empowerment, there is no need for a priestly class or Church tradition. Hence, authority since the 1970's has become more decentralized. "Leadership is often based on personal charisma rather than on formal bureaucratic training within an institutional hierarchy. This movement's most characteristic form is the small prayer group and the "covenant community," which has minimal structure so that it can remain open to the Spirit and provide intimate support for its members."[231] Here, the dissenting, antiauthoritarian streak in Protestantism has run full course.

A paper dealing with new religious movements written by Roy Wallis, "Reflections on When Prophecy Fails," contains an observation that could easily apply to both the New Age and Pentecostal/charismatic movements:

> First there prevails in the milieu an attitude of "epistemological individualism," that is, a belief that the individual is the ultimate locus for the determination of truth. Secondly, there prevails an ideology of "revelational indeterminacy," that is, a belief that the truth may be revealed in diverse ways and through diverse

agents. No individual or collectivity possesses a monopoly of the truth.[232]

The New Age movement has made major inroads among the Roman Catholic population. "The vast majority of people most interested in New Age thought — 81% — continue to identify with Roman Catholicism (53%) or Protestantism (28%).[233] While these figures are for Canada, I do not think the U.S. is much different. In her book *Ungodly Rage: The Hidden Face of Catholic Feminism*, conservative Catholic journalist and author Donna Steichen reveals how many nuns are now unabashedly employing New Age practices in their spiritual life (e.g., tarot cards, crystals, dream work, and rebirth rituals).[234] Steichen records the early skepticism of Roman Catholics toward stories of nuns involving themselves in the occult, and her own first confrontation with it:

> Like their secular contemporaries, American Catholics were sure, not only that witchcraft was outmoded, but that it had never existed at all outside the imaginations of misogynist clergymen and superstitious peasants. But as feminist extremists seized and maintained control of religious houses, the unimaginable became a reality.
>
> Early rumors of excesses among the nuns were dismissed as distasteful and flatly incredible except by the few who encountered them firsthand. At my own first exposure to witchcraft, I

thought I had stumbled into a uniquely lunatic social cul-de-sac. I didn't know it was part of a movement and didn't guess how closely it was entangled with general theological dissent, broader political feminism, and epidemic neo-gnosticism. Later investigation revealed that witchcraft is one particularly bizarre manifestation of a widely disseminated decay. Most of the old Catholic culture has been devoured by spiritual termites, leaving behind a structure that looks solid to the eye but crumbles at the touch.[235]

Steichen quotes feminist nun Sister Madonna Kolbenschlag, who predicts that the church she has consecrated herself to will "whither away" in the presence of a new spirituality:

The sign of ultimate religious experience will surely be . . . its power to release truly spiritual redemptive energies. . . . In this "truly catholic" New Faith . . . the Church will wither away, made unnecessary by the direct illumination of "a creative Spiritual Presence that comes from *within* them as well as from *beyond*. . . . Experience will replace revelation as the ground of moral judgment. . . . The New Faith obliterates patriarchal theology and the Church."[236]

Observations

We should always try to visualize the end results as we pray. . . . If you have not visualized
clearly in your heart exactly what you hope for,
it cannot become a reality to you. . . . We have
taught our people how to . . . visualize success. .
. . Through visualizing and dreaming, you can
incubate your future and hatch the results.

—Word-Faith   Preacher
Paul Yonggi Cho[237]

Thus saith the Lord of hosts; Hearken not to the
words of the prophets that prophesy to you,
and deceive you: they speak a vision of their
own heart, and not out of the mouth of the
Lord.

—Jeremiah 23:16

Money and the love of it carry with it an enormous
spiritual danger ("for where thy treasure is, there is thy
heart also" —Matt. 6:21), which is why it is mentioned
in the Bible twice as many times as faith and prayer
combined. In fact, Jesus has more to say about money
than heaven and hell. Being wealthy is not a sin, as evidenced by the righteous men of wealth recorded in the
Bible (e.g., Abraham, Job, Jesus' friend Lazarus, and Joseph of Arimathea). God does not condemn material
wealth, only the inordinate attachment to it.

And every man to whom God hath given riches, and substance, and hath given him power to eat thereof, and to enjoy his portion, and to rejoice of his labor: this is the gift of God (Eccles. 5:18).

What is perverse is the "name it and claim it"/"prosperity gospel" preached by the tele-evangelists of Word-Faith ministry beamed from Trinity Broadcasting Network. Perverse because they inject the New Age occult practice of "creative visualization, employed by human potential seminars such as Silva Mind Control, est (Erhard Seminars Training and Mind Dynamics),[238] into the most sacred area of Christianity: prayer. "Creative Visualization" is explained in an Amway motivational tape by Crown Direct Distributor Bunny Marks entitled "What You See Is What You'll Be":

So the first thing we must do if we wish to achieve and live the life of success, the life of plenty and happiness, is first of all to visualize it.

We actually create reality by what we visualize. . . .

The picture you hold in your mind will develop the same way a film develops. . . . If you start visualizing what you desire, you shall have it! You can have anything you desire if you want it badly enough and begin to visualize it. . . . So the picture's the secret, that is the key; for *the picture you hold is the picture you'll be!*[239]

Word-Faith preacher Paul Yonggi Cho advises people on the use of "creative visualization" in their prayer life:

> We should always try to visualize the end result as we pray. . . . If you have not visualized clearly in your heart exactly what you hope for, it cannot become a reality to you. . . .
>
> We have taught our people how to . . . visualize success. . . . Through visualizing and dreaming, you can incubate your future and hatch the results.[240]

By grossly distorting Mark 10:30, Word-Faith preacher Kenneth Copeland's wife, Gloria, completely inverts the Christian motive of charitable giving to that of avarice:

> You give $1 for the Gospel's sake and $100 belongs to you; give $10 and receive $1000; give $1000 and receive $100,000. I know that you can multiply, but I want you to see it in black and white and see how tremendous the hundredfold return is. . . . Give one house and receive one hundred houses or one house worth a hundred times as much. Give one airplane and receive one hundred times the value of the airplane. Give one car and the return would furnish you with a lifetime of cars. In short, Mark 10:30 is a very good deal.[241]

This is all particularly distressing when we realize the enormous growth of churches associated with the

Positive Confession, or Word-Faith movement, aided by the media dominance of the Trinity Broadcasting Network and their tele-evangelists. God descended into humanity to die an agonizing death on a cross in order to save us from our sins and destroy death, not to reveal a sacred power that can be manipulated and gained by using mind-power techniques — "creative visualization," correct word formula, etc. The faith of the "name it and claim it/prosperity gospel" is not a humble faith in God's Divine Providence. Rather, it is a presumptuous, formal, legalistic faith that projects "mind power" at God, whom is then believed compelled to deliver our prayer request.[242]

This belief in a divine, sacred metaphysical power that can be tapped into in order to achieve infinite potential is very similar to the Third and Fourth insights found in *The Celestine Prophecy:* "The Third and Fourth had showed me that the universe was in reality a vast system of energy and that human conflict was a shortage of and a manipulation for this energy." Also, on the dust jacket we read: "Most exciting of all, you can explore a deeper connection with your own personal energy and divine source." Pastor Robert Schuller couldn't agree more: "You don't know what power you have within you! . . . You can make your world into anything you choose. Yes, you can make your world into whatever you want it to be" and "Now — Believe and You Will Achieve."[243]

The adoption by large numbers of Christians of the "name it and claim it/prosperity gospel" of the human potential/New Age movement will wreak destruction on their faith. In their pursuit of wealth and success, they should turn off the tele-evangelists and pause just long enough to ponder Christ's warning to the Laodiceans—a people also preoccupied with material wealth:

> So then, because you are lukewarm, and neither cold nor hot, I will vomit you out of my mouth. Because you say, "I am rich, have become wealthy, and have need of nothing (Revelation 3:16–17, NKJV).

CHAPTER SEVEN

Christianity's Great Challenge

We do not want a church that will move with the world. We want a church that will move the world.

— G. K. Chesterton

The culture-forming energies of Christianity depend upon the church's ability to resist the temptation to become completely identified with, or absorbed into, the culture.

— Christopher Dawson

The New Age movement thrives in our pluralistic society, which openly accepts and tolerates a wide variety of lifestyles, moralities, and a large pantheon of gods enjoying equal validity. This kind of plurality, of course, only serves to erode and undermine the legitimacy and moral authority of any one particular religious body. For in this relativistic environment, claiming one god to be true at the expense of the others is seen as arrogant, bigoted, intolerant, offensive, and anti-democratic. At a large American university, students were asked if they believed in an absolute truth that transcended time and diverse cultures. They responded as follows:

"Truth is whatever you believe."

"There is no absolute truth."

"If there were such a thing as absolute truth, how could we know what it was?"

"People who believe in absolute truth are dangerous."[244]

According to Elliot Miller, New Agers believe "it is the height of presumption to think that one knows the key truth for all people. On the other hand, it is the apex of love to 'allow' others to have their own 'truth,' 'thou shalt not interfere with another's reality' might be called the First Commandment of New Age revelation."[245] Truth relativism is a key belief of the New Age movement; its adoption by large numbers of Christians and their resultant "consumer" mentality towards religion will be explored in this chapter.

A 1990 national survey of Canadian adults found that some "65% endorse the idea that 'everything is relative.' In addition, no less that 50% maintain that what is right or wrong is a matter of personal opinion."[246] Pollster George Barna reveals that these figures are very much in line with Americans, where 66% claim disbelief in absolute truth. Barna shows that these figures do not improve very much with U.S. evangelicals, who are inconsistent and contradictory when it comes to the question of absolute truth. For while 88% of those polled affirmed the Bible as the infallible word of God, 53% denied the existence of absolute truth. Barna's work further revealed that "among the people groups most ardently supportive of this viewpoint are mainline

Protestants."[247] This kind of truth relativism is necessary in order to sustain the existence of the spiritual consumer. This is a distressing aspect of our postmodern society, especially when found among Christians, as sociologist Reginald W. Bibby reveals in his book *Fragmented Gods*.[248]

Religious Consumers

. . . a supermarket of faiths, received, jazzed-up, homespun, restored, imported and exotic. But all of them co-exist because the wider society is so secular, because they are relatively unimportant consumer items.[249]

Bibby, by posing the age-old question "Did the gods create us, or did we create the gods?," draws a comprehensive portrait of religion in contemporary Canada (observations that are equally valid for the U.S.) shows that "for some time now, a highly specialized, consumer-oriented society has been remolding the gods. . . . Consumers tell religion what type of religion they would like; culture accordingly tells religion how to update and upgrade its content and forms."[250] Instead of reminding culture that churches have creeds, dogmas, traditions, and values that transcend culture, many churches respond by asking, "What would you like a church to be?" The net result, of course, is that they then join the ranks with all other consumer goods and services. The results of such pandering are predictable, as Bibby correctly points out: "Ironically, in trying to get in step with the modern age, organized religion—

by dismantling the gods and serving them up piece-meal—is running the risk of becoming increasingly trivial."[251]

A prime example of "becoming increasingly trivial" is an ad placed by a Christian group in *Common Ground*, a Vancouver, British Columbia, New Age newspaper in 1993. The ad was listed under "Spiritual Practices" and shared space with the Sufi Order, Shambhala Training, Johrei, and the Zen Center. The ad assured non-Christian readers in the following terms:

> WARRANTY. Many people are attracted to Christ—it's Christians who give them trouble. If you attend our church, WE PROMISE not to tell you how to dress, feel, think, or vote. We won't discourage your questions or insult your intelligence. WE PROMISE to welcome you in Christ's name, involve you in our community if you like, or leave you in peace if you'd prefer. WE PROMISE to smile now and then, experiencing with you the joy of life in Christ. If we breach this promise, you are entitled to reclaim your misgivings about "organized religion." Kitsilano Christian Community meets Sundays at 9:30 at 1708 West 16th Ave., and in small groups all over the place during the week.[252]

The consumer mentality toward religion is already evident in much of Protestantism—even among conservatives who regard much of modern culture with disdain. As Bibby observes:

Their church-shopping tendencies epitomize a consumer attitude toward religion. In looking for the "true" gospel, the "right" version of the Bible, "good" music, "biblical preaching," "warm fellowship," and so on, the Conservative Protestant—like so many people in other religious groups—becomes a customer in search of a product.[253]

Doctrinal differences pose no barriers for these spiritual consumers, for these seekers will move from Anglican (Episcopal), to Baptist, to Lutheran, to Pentecostal, to Evangelical churches. Now, all these churches are in substantial disagreement on Guaranteed Salvation, Baptism, Infant Baptism, Perpetual Virginity of Mary, the Eucharist, etc. These are all less important than good preaching, "good music," and "warm fellowship."

Andrew Walker, the Orthodox director of the C. S. Lewis Centre and honorary fellow of King's College, London, laments the consumer "supermarket" approach of contemporary Christianity:

Christianity is now on sale in multiform shapes and sizes. Competing in the open market with other religions, there is a bewildering yet broad choice of "real" and "best" Christianities for anyone who wants to buy. No doubt someone will soon publish "The Consumer's Guide to God" so that people can pop in and out of churches with the same ease and comfort as they visit their favourite restaurants.[254]

The Disaster of Truth Relativism

If God were to hold out enclosed in His right hand all Truth, and in His left hand just the active search for Truth, though with the condition that I should ever err therein, and should say to me: Choose! I should humbly take His left hand and say: Father! Give me this one; absolute Truth belongs to Thee alone.

—G. E. Lessing[255]

The current state of objective truth is well illustrated in the "Dear Abby" column that dealt with religious differences within families. A reader wrote to Abby:

Your answer to the woman who complained that her relatives were always arguing with her about religion was ridiculous. You advised her to simply declare the subject off-limits. Are you suggesting that people talk only about trivial, meaningless subjects so as to avoid a potential controversy? . . . It is arrogant to tell people there are subjects they may not mention in your presence. You could have suggested she learn enough about her relatives' cult to show them the errors contained in its teachings.

Abby replied:

In my view, the height of arrogance is to attempt to show people the 'errors' in the religion of their choice.[256]

Abby's response mirrors society's distrust and alienation towards those who claim objectivity. For to claim objective truth, especially in religion, is to show oneself to be a narrow-minded, intolerant bigot, and perhaps even dangerous.

Another example is as follows: Let's say you're at a party and you're engaged in a discussion about abortion with one of the guests. While you claim it's a moral evil, the guest, being pro-abortion, sees nothing wrong with it. Just as you're warming to your case and developing some telling points, along comes a relativist with a smile on his face and a drink in his hand. "You two have quite a discussion going here." You explain the discussion to the relativist and tell him that, medically, scientifically, and philosophically, a fetus or pre-born infant is fully human and, therefore, the taking of that life constitutes a moral evil. "Yeah," he says, "interesting point; you've obviously given it a lot of thought. Yes, I can certainly see that this is your value. Well, the pro-life position is true for you." He then turns to the other guest, still smiling, "And what's your position?" The other guest tells him that with abortion we are only dealing with pre-human tissue that does not enjoy personhood and is, therefore, morally neutral. "Yes," replies our relativist, "then that is your value—that's true for you. Where's the problem?"

This, of course, is nothing more than intellectual suicide, for as I mentioned in Chapter 1, the claim that there is no objective truth is pure nonsense. For the immediate response to such an absolute statement asserting the nonexistence of truth would be to ask if that were true. Thus, the silly statement ends up proving the truth it attempt to negate. However, what passes today for modern wisdom is one of the oldest philosophies known to man.

In fifth-century Athens, there were philosophers known as Sophists who taught that truth was purely relative. They didn't say, "true for you" — they stated their case more elegantly. They began with the doctrine of Heraclitus that all things change. Human beings and all living creatures ingest nutrients and pass through a life cycle. There is constant change. All of creation is in constant flux. Therefore, if all living matter is not static and unchangeable, it must follow that there can be no unchangeable truth. Everything we learn is through sense perception. Due to constant change, no two people see the same thing, because what they see is always changing; consequently, every individual has a right to his own opinion — one opinion is as good as another. The world perceived by each individual is his own reality. Contradictory statements can both be true. Man is the measure of all things. Since there is no absolute truth, morality is determined by custom, and it follows, therefore, that the crowd is always right.

Socrates was appalled by the teaching of the Sophists. He saw them as destroying the underlying principles of morality. He taught that unchangeable truth is a reality (e.g., if 100,000 people shouted from the rooftops that adultery and stealing were right, it would not make it so). Well, before the advent of Christianity, sophistry fell into disrepute. Even up until a hundred years ago, it was quite common to see characters in

136

novels having their clever but fallacious arguments being dismissed as "pure sophistry."

University of Chicago professor Allan Bloom blames the current educational system for the indoctrination of truth relativism:

> There is one thing a professor can be absolutely certain of: almost every student entering the university believes, or says he believes, that truth is relative. If this belief is put to the test, one can count on the students' reaction: they will be uncomprehending. That anyone should regard the proposition as not self-evident astonishes them, as though he were calling into question 2+2=4. These are things you don't think about. . . . They are unified only in their relativism and in their allegiance to equality. And the two are related in a moral intention. The relativity of truth is not a theoretical insight but a moral postulate, the condition of a free society, or so they see it. . . . The danger they have been taught to fear from absolutism is not error but intolerance. Relativism is necessary to openness; and this is the virtue, the only virtue, which all primary education for more than fifty years has dedicated itself to inculcating. Openness—and the relativism that makes it the only plausible stance in the face of various claims to truth and various ways of life and kinds of human beings—is the great insight of our times. The true believer is the real danger. The study of history and of culture teaches that all the

world was mad in the past; men always thought they were right, and that led to wars, persecutions, slavery, xenophobia, racism, and chauvinism. The point is not to correct the mistakes and be really right; rather it is not to think you are right at all.[257]

Professor Bloom goes on to say that when challenged, "The students, of course, cannot defend their opinion."[258] For instance, he asks them if they had been a British administrator in India, would they have banned *suttee,* the Hindu practice of burning widows alive on their husband's funeral pyre. Would they impose their Judeo-Christian Eurocentric values on these people? Bloom comments that they "either remain silent or reply that the British should never have been there in the first place."[259]

It is little wonder that the New Age movement flourishes in this irrational environment that claims truth and morality are relative and not absolute. For in order to create their own realities, New Agers have to deny absolutes. Thus, when all values are then subordinated to their own personal preferences, the Romantic quest for inward focus, displacement of reason in favor of emotion, and intuition is realized. Shirley MacLaine can then declare, "That's my reality. So no one can say whether my reality is correct or not."[260] If we accept truth relativism, then she is absolutely right. However, the New Age movement — like all Romantic movements before — will soon pass from the scene.

CHRISTIANITY'S GREAT CHALLENGE

New Age Occultism
and the Temptation to Power

You can have what you say! In fact, what you are saying is exactly what you are getting now.

— Kenneth Copeland[261]

The chief distinguishing feature of the New Age movement is the temptation, or will to power (i.e., the personal empowerment of the individual to create one's own reality — "every individual is fundamentally the creator and the controller of his own destiny . . . you must continually remember your Divinity and, most important, act accordingly").[262] New Agers will use creative visualization and other human potential techniques plus astrology, tarot cards, mediums, and spirit guides to gain control over the immediate present and the future. There is no personal God to whom they are morally accountable to, only an impersonal force or energy to be manipulated for their own ends.

At the urging of many pastors, numerous Christians are falling into the personal empowerment trap with "creative visualization," "positive confession," "name it, claim it." In doing so, they slide unconsciously into the occult. For the heart of the New Age, Word-Faith "creative visualization"/"positive confession"/"name it, claim it" movement is the belief that what we say and how hard we visualize the object of our prayer is less important than our faith in prayer. It all comes down to technique — a legalistic formula where if you apply the right words with enough visual imaging, God will be *required* to deliver "the goods."

139

With the aid of New Age occultic practices, an unheard-of formalistic, legal relationship with God is introduced. Armed with this unbelievable presumption, a Christian is filled with a tremendous feeling of personal empowerment, because he now believes and insists that when the correct wording is addressed to God, He has to deliver. As Word-Faith preacher Kenneth Copeland assures us:

> *You can have what you say!* In fact, what you are saying is exactly what you are getting now. If you are living in poverty and lack of want, change what you are saying. It will change what you have. . . . Discipline your vocabulary. Discipline everything you do, everything you say, everything you think to agree with what God does, what God says, and what God thinks. God will be obligated to meet your needs because of His word. . . . If you stand firmly on this, your needs will be met.[263]

This is a far cry from the humble submission to God's will that has always been the hallmark of Christian character. Compare this with the following biblical injunctions on the correct approach to God and prayer:

> For if any man think himself to be something, whereas he is nothing, he deceiveth himself (Gal. 6:3).

> He hath regard to the prayer of the humble: and he hath not despised their petition (Psalm 101:18).

For he that hath been humbled shall be in glory: and he that shall bow down his eyes, he shall be saved (Job 22:29).

The Lord is nigh unto them that are of a contrite heart: and He will save the humble of spirit (Psalm 33:19).

God is a loving Father who knows us better than ourselves and will, therefore, provide us with what we really need, rather than what we think we need and will "do all things more abundantly than we desire or understand" (Eph. 3:20). This is vastly different from an occultic type of faith in God that insists He has to always deliver what exactly we want. The Christian leaders who preach this twisted faith to their flock are guilty of sowing weeds in the good field (Matt. 13:28) and, in doing so, "taketh the word out of their heart"(Luke 8:12).

The promise of New Age occultism is power — the power to control our own destiny. This has always been the promise of the occult, and it is this inherent refusal to submit to the authority of God that makes it evil.

The reality of life is spiritual, and the great battleground is the human heart, as the great Russian writer Alexander Solzhenhytsin discovered while incarcerated in a Soviet gulag:

And it was only when I lay there on rotting straw that I sensed within myself the first stirrings of good. Gradually it was disclosed to me that the line separating good and evil passes not through states, nor between classes, nor be-tween political parties either—but right through every human heart—and through all human hearts.[264]

That evil is a spiritual reality of which St. Paul warns the Ephesians:

For our wrestling is not against flesh and blood; but against principalities and powers, against the rulers of the world of this darkness, against the spirits of wickedness in high places. (Eph. 6:12)

Evil is a negative power that lacks any positive at-tributes, and it exists only to negate and destroy its op-posite—good. It is like a parasite that can only exist by attaching itself to that which is good and draining it of its essence. It despises the nature on which it preys and, like a cancer, it can only grow by devouring and de-stroying the moral character of its host. While promis-ing freedom and power, the occult always ends up by bringing its adherents into some form of bondage as Helena Blavatsky discovered:

I would gladly return, I would gladly be Rus-sian, Christian, Orthodox. I yearn for it. But there is no returning; I am in chains; I am not my own."[265]

The Demise of the New Age Movement

When society once again embraces rationality and objectivity—as it always does—we are going to look even sillier than our Victorian forebears. As I mentioned in the Introduction, the key to understanding the New Age phenomenon is twofold. First, to recognize that irrational, esoteric, religious movements are as old as humanity and intensify during periods of alienation and anxiety. Second, that this is truly a Romantic Movement—in its displacement of reason by intuition and emotion, its fixation with the supernatural and the paranormal, and its belief that the way to all mysteries lead inward to the human ego bear its unmistakable marks. This, combined with its eclectic, exotic, indiscriminate mix of crystal power, pyramid power, spirit channeling, spirit guides, reincarnation, auras, telepathy, extraterrestrial revelations, etc., creates a highly unstable compound that will deny it any permanence as a religious movement.

All the great religions of the world that have created enduring civilizations (e.g., Judaism, Christianity, and Islam) have belief systems rooted in absolutes that deal with the central questions of life. They speak with authority and a moral vision on the perplexities, suffering, and ultimate meaning of the human experience. By contrast, the New Age movement lacks a fixed coherent system of values and absolutes that can be passed on as a distinct religious culture through countless generations. Its only chance of long-term survival seems largely tied to its ability to insinuate itself into the general culture by providing a unified worldview and way of life for its adherents. This would involve the development of New Age organizations and even churches, which would rival or surpass traditional church organizations in drawing power, cohesiveness, and retention of membership. It would also involve the successful infiltration of Christian churches with New Age theology.

Noted historian Christopher Lasch sees the New Age as "lacking the religious backbone to pull this off."[266] It is true, as we have seen, that the New Age movement has been successful in infiltrating some Christian churches with its ideas. However, Lasch claims that its success will be short lived, because New Age teaching lacks that necessary "submission to a body of teachings that has to be accepted even when it conflicts with immediate interests or inclinations and cannot constantly be redesigned to individual specifications." He believes that the truth relativity of "It's true if you believe it" is "appealing in the short run, but in the long run it works no wonders."[267]

When society once again embraces rationality and objectivity—as it always does—we are going to look even sillier than our Victorian forebears, with their spiritualistic parlor games and table rapping. It is going to be very embarrassing to look back at society's infatuation with crystal power, pyramid power, spirit channeling, spirit guides, reincarnation, auras, telepathy, extraterrestrial revelations, etc. What will they make of the likes of Shirley MacLaine: "I'm learning to look into the future (through mind traveling), and if I want to change it, I can."[268] Or, "If you don't see me as God, it's because you don't see yourself as God."[269]

The real tragedy in this postmodern New Age, Romantic movement are the churches that so quickly capitulated to what they thought was an irresistible wave of new spiritual insights and discoveries instead of seeing it for what it really is: a rehash of gnosticism, nineteenth-century spiritualism, and Eastern mysticism.

The spiritual truths of Christianity transcend culture and, therefore, can only maintain moral authority and act as society's conscience when it stands above and against culture. When churches join in the latest whims and infatuations of popular culture, they quickly become irrelevant, descending to the level of other spiritual commodities to be picked over, consumed, and discarded at will.

Just as the mystery religions of the Roman Empire could not satisfy the spiritual longings of her citizens, so the New Age movement, with its exotic, eclectic, supermarket variety spirituality, cannot in the long term satisfy the spiritual hunger of our postmodern society. This is just as true for the counterfeit, tinsel and glitter, "name it, claim it" Christianity offered by the tele-evangelists. Genuine Christianity will triumph, because it speaks with an authoritative voice to the deep, perplexing questions that confound all human beings as they journey through life. Rather than offering trivial, shallow, easy, and attractive solutions to the enormous moral and emotional challenges of human existence, it charges it with profound religious meaning.

Christ's answer to the enigma of human experience is noble and majestic, void of soft options: "If any man will come after me, let him take up his cross and follow me. For he that will lose his life for my sake shall find it" (Matt. 16:24–25). The modern mind finds these sayings grotesque. It's just too difficult to believe, that true joy and understanding can be found in self-sacrifice and detachment. However, the wisdom of Christ will be rediscovered and cherished again when the counterfeit gods of our anxious age betray us. For those who look at societal decay and despair of any reformation, it is one of the lessons of history that civilizations can renew themselves. It is also a great lesson of history that while many things are probable, nothing is inevitable; and, with God, of course everything is possible. Let us all ardently pray for the rebirth of a Christian society.

GLOSSARY OF NEW AGE TERMS

Age of Aquarius: Aquarius is a large constellation representing a man pouring water from a jar and is the eleventh sign of the zodiac. Astrologers claim that every 2,000 to 2,400 years, we move from one sign of the zodiac to another. The current cycle has taken us from Pisces to Aquarius. Hence, the Aquarian Age ushering in the era of enlightened man celebrated in the popular song:

> This is the dawning of the Age of Aquarius! Harmony and understanding, sympathy and trust abounding, no more falsehoods or derision, golden living dreams of visions, mystic crystal revelation, and the mind's true liberation. Aquarius! Aquarius! Aquarius!

Akashik Records: Believed to be a vast scroll house of omniscient knowledge of all that has ever been, including the histories of all human lives, stored in ethereal energy.

Ascended Masters or **Spirit Guides:** Departed souls whose past lifetimes have elevated them to the highest plateau of spiritual growth and beyond the necessity for further reincarnations. They now permanently inhabit the spiritual realm, ready to be channeled through an appointed medium and reveal the mysteries of life.

Astral: A suspended state where, after death, people go to await further reincarnation.

Astral Projection: An out-of-body experience that is claimed to occur while being fully conscious, one's spiritual entity floats free from the physical body while remaining attached by a thin, umbilical-like cord.

Attunement: A New Age form of prayer called at-one-ment, which refers to the belief that total union with God can be achieved.

Aura: Colors radiating from the body indicating the spiritual or psychological condition of the person.

Avatar: A Hindu term for the descent in human form of a deity or soul to give spiritual direction to people. Christ, Buddha, and Krishna are considered avatars who have spiritually progressed to the point that further reincarnation to work off bad karma in unnecessary.

Channeling: Another way the realm of the occult communicates its "secrets" is by speaking through a person endowed with special powers (e.g., a medium or channeler), who passively allows (by going into a trance) disembodied spirits to take control of his body in order to impart their wisdom.

Cosmic Christ: The Christ of the New Age is a cosmic energy or universal spirit, who with his occultic wisdom will enlighten us and lead us to the self-realization of our own divinity.

Harmonic Convergence: Relates to a global event in 1987, where "critical mass" was attempted by New Agers gathering in different points on the globe according to favorable astrological time, in order to usher in a higher state of consciousness and world peace.

Karma: A Buddhist and Hindu term, referring to the sum total of a person's good and evil deeds in a previous state of existence, that will decide his or her state in a future existence. (See *Reincarnation*)

Monism: Denies the duality of matter and mind and claims that all creation originates from a single divine source.

Pantheism: (Greek *pan*, "all," *Theos*, "God") Pantheism asserts that God is not a Being with personality who contemplates His creation from the outside. Rather, God is only identifiable with the forces of nature, thus the infinite demarcation between the Creator and His creation dissolves into a cosmic oneness — All is God, All is One.

Reincarnation: The idea of a continuous cycle of death and rebirth in another body until one has worked off all the bad karma and attained spiritual perfection. (See *Karma*)

Tarot Cards: A deck of seventy-eight playing cards used in fortune telling and decorated with pictures of the devil, sun, moon, the Egyptian goddess Isis, etc.

Theosophy: In 1875, Helena Blavatsky, together with the American Colonel Henry Steel Olcott, founded the Theosophical Society in New York, an international group of occultists who claimed that reincarnation was the path to a purified humanity. They also undertook to conduct a comparative study of world religions and to form a universal brotherhood of man.

Visualization or **Guided Imagery:** The belief that we can create objective reality by the power of highly concentrated thought — literally, "mind over matter."

NOTES

1. *The Report,* December 20, 1999, p. 39.

2. Caryl Matrisciana, *Gods of the New Age* (Eugene, Oregon: Harvest House Publishers, 1985), pp. 17–18.

3. Irving Hexham, "The Evangelical Response to the New Age," in James R. Lewis and J. Gordon Melton, eds., *Perspectives on the New Age* (State University of New York Press, 1992), p. 157.

4. Michael F. Brown, *The Channeling Zone: American Spirituality in an Anxious Age* (Cambridge, Massachusetts: Harvard University Press, 1997), p. 7.

5. Oswald Spengler, *The Decline of the West,* vol. 2 (New York: Alfred A. Knopf, Inc., 1980), p. 310.

6. Shirley MacLaine, *Dancing in the Light* (Toronto: Bantam Books, 1985), p. 326.

7. Kenneth Clark, *Civilisation* (New York: Harper & Row, 1969), p. 347.

8. Susan Love Brown, "Baby Boomers, American Character, and the New Age," in *Perspectives on the New Age,* p. 90.

9. Charles E. Strickland and Andrew M. Ambrose, "The Baby Boom, Prosperity, and the Changing Worlds of Children, 1945–1963" in Joseph M. Hawkes and N. Ray Hiner, eds, *American Childhood: A Research Guide and Historical Handbook* (Westport, Connecticut: Greenwood Press, 1985), pp. 533–585.

10. Brown, p. 91.

11. Strickland and Ambrose, *Ibid.*

12. Daniel Yankelovich, *New Rules: Searching for Self-Fulfillment in a World Turned Upside Down* (New York: Random House, 1981) p. 4.

13. *Ibid.,* p. 5.

14. *Ibid.*

15. *Time,* Dec. 7, 1987, p. 68.

16. Reginald W. Bibby, *Unknown Gods* (Toronto: Stoddart Publishing Company, 1993), p. 49.

17. *The Report,* December 20, 1999, p. 36.

18. *Time* (December 7, 1987), p. 66.

19. Cited in Bibby.

20. *L'Osservatore Romano,* English edition, May 14, 1990, p. 2.

21. James Redfield, *The Celestine Prophecy: An Experiential Guide* (New York: Warner Books, 1995), p. 270.

22. James Redfield, *The Celestine Prophecy* (New York: Warner Books, 1993).

23. *Newsweek* (June 24, 1996), Vol. 127 Issue 26, p. 70.

24. James Redfield, *The Celestine Prophecy,* pp. 34–35.

25. *Ibid.,* p. 241.

26. James Redfield, *The Celestine Prophecy: An Experiential Guide* (New York: Warner Books, 1995).

27. Shirley MacLaine, *Dancing in the Light,* p. 357.

28. Shirley MacLaine, *Out on a Limb* (New York: Bantam Books, 1986), p. 16.

29. *Ibid.,* p.202.

30. *Ibid.,* p. 182.

31. *Ibid.,* p. 187.

32. *Ibid.,* pp. 198, 204, 209.

33. *Ibid.,* pp. 199–200.

34. *Ibid.,* p. 203.

35. *Ibid.,* p. 328.

36. *Ibid.,* p. 367.

37. F. LaGard Smith, *Out on a Broken Limb* (Eugene, Oregon: Harvest House Publishers, 1986), p.102.

38. *Ibid.,* p.103.

39. *Ibid.*

40. Henry Gordon, *Channeling into the New Age* (Buffalo, New York: 1988), p. 134.

41. Shirley MacLaine, *It's All in the Playing* (New York: Bantam Books, 1987), p. 192.

42. *Ibid.,* p. 136.

43. *Time,* Dec. 7, 1987, p. 67.

44. *The Phil Donahue Show,* Sept. 14, 1987, as quoted by Gordon.

45. *Time,* Dec. 7, 1987, p. 68.

46. David W. Hoover, *How to Respond to the Occult* (St. Louis: Concordia Publishing House, 1977), p. 8.

47. Redfield, pp. 34–35.

48. *Out on a Limb*, p. 209.

49. *The Problems of Modern Society*, edited by Peter Worsley (Harmondsworth, Middlesex, England: Penguin Books, 1978), Martin Marty, *The Occult Establishment*, p. 747.

50. To the Countess of Upper Ossory, 16 August, 1776.

51. James Webb, *The Occult Establishment* (LaSalle, Illinois: Open Court, 1991), p. 8.

52. *Superstition.*

53. T.H. Huxley, *Biogenesis and Abiogenesis*, p. viii.

54. *Pensees*, 224 [11-277].

55. To Benjamin Bailey, Nov. 22, 1817.

56. Norman Davies, *Europe: A History* (London: Pimlico, 1997), p. 783.

57. C. S. Lewis, *A Pilgrim's Regress* (London: Bles, 1943), p. 12.

58. *The Brontes: Twentieth Century Views* (Englewood Cliffs, New Jersey: Prentice Hall, 1970), p. 76.

59. Russell Chandler, *Understanding the New Age* (Dallas: Word Publishing, 1988), pp. 146–147.

60. Jack Underhill, "New Age Quiz," *Life Times Magazine,* no. 3, 6.

61. Douglas R. Groothuis, *Unmasking the New Age* (Downers Grove, Illinois: Varsity Press, 1986), p. 79.

62. "New Age Movement," Microsoft Encarta Online, Encyclopaedia 2000, encarta.msn.com.

63. *Encounters with the Paranormal,* Kendrick Frazier, ed. (Amherst, New York: Prometheus Books, 1998), pp. 246, 248.

64. Ibid., pp. 223–224.

65. Dave Hunt and T. A. McMahon, *America: The Sorcerer's New Apprentice* (Eugene, Oregon: Harvest House Publishers, 1988), p. 170.

66. *Ibid.,* p. 264.

67. *New York Times,* July 21, 1997, p. B1.

68. *Encounters with the Paranormal,* p. 265.

69. *New York Times,* July 21, 1997, pp. B1–B4.

70. Gordon, p. 51.

71. Bob Larson, *Straight Answers on the New Age* (Nashville, Tennessee: Thomas Nelson, 1989), p. 20.

72. Cited in Glenn A. Rupert, "Employing the New Age: Training Seminars," in *Perspectives on the New Age,* p. 128.

73. *Ibid.,* p. 20. Also Wellspring Retreat and Resource Center, *The Siren Call of Modern Pied Pipers,* www.wellspring.albany.oh.us.

74. Elliot Miller, *A Crash Course on the New Age Movement* (Grand Rapids, Michigan: Baker Book House, 1989), p.100. Cited in Rupert, p. 127.

75. *Time*, Dec. 7, 1987, pp. 66–67.

76. Miller, p. 100.

77. Chandler, p. 29.

78. Gertrude Himmelfarb, *De-Moralization of Society* (New York: Vintage Books, 1994), p. 188.

79. Cited in Ruth A. Tucker, *Another Gospel: Alternative Religions and the New Age Movement* (Grand Rapids, Michigan: Academie Books, 1989), p. 330.

80. McMahon, "MLA Selling Controversial Training," *Calgary Herald,* January 14, 1983, p. A1.

81. Cited in Larson, p. 239.

82. Cited in Tucker, p. 330.

83. Malcolm Muggeridge, *Tread Softly for you Tread on my Jokes* (London and Glasgow: Fontana Books, 1972), p. 16.

84. Russell Chandler, pp. 147–148.

85. Cited in Rupert, p. 131.

86. Rupert, p. 131.

87. Cited in Rupert, p. 131.

88. Groothuis, p.160.

89. Wellspring, *The Siren Call of Modern Pied Pipers.*

90. *Ibid.* Also see Larson, p. 21, and Chandler, p. 150.

91. *Time,* Dec. 7, 1987, pp. 66–67.

92. Chandler, p. 163.

93. *Ibid.,* pp. 164–165.

94. worldworks@lifematters.com

95. www.network.uk/~asclepius/choosing-your-crystals

96. *Dancing in the Light,* p. 8.

97. *The Langley Advance News,* Tuesday, April 25, 2000, p. 11.

98. Cited by MacLaine, *Out on a Limb,* p. 356.

99. Gerald R. Cragg, *The Church and the Age of Reason* (London: Penguin Books, 1990), p. 283.

100. Douglas R. Groothuis, *Unmasking the New Age,* p. 82.

101. *Ibid.,* pp. 82–83.

102. Douglas R. Groothuis, *Countering the New Age,* p. 203.

103. *Ideas,* Geoffrey Grigson & Charles Harvard Gibbs-Smith, gen. ed. (New York: Hawthorne Books), p. 286.

104. *Inscriptiones Graecae ad Res Romanas Pertinentes* (Paris, 1906–1927), vol. 1, No. 117, as quoted in *Roman Civilization,* vol. 11, Naphtali Lewis & Meyer Reinhold,

ed. (New York: Columbia University Press, 1967), p. 570.

105. *The Report*, "It's 50 B.C. All Over Again," Dec. 20, 1999, p. 37.

106. Cambridge Latin Course, Unit 3, The North American Third Edition, Ed Phinney, Patricia E. Bell, Barbara Romaine, ed. (New York: Press Syndicate of the University of Cambridge, 1997), p. 51.

107. D. M. Field, *Roman and Greek Mythology* (London: The Hamlyn Publishing Group Limited, 1977), p. 182.

108. *The Report*, p. 37.

109. Cicero, *ad fam.* xiv, 4, 1, as quoted by R. T. Glover, *The Conflict of Religions in the Roman Empire* (London: Methuen & Co. Ltd., 1923), p. 10.

110. Charles Norris Cochrane, *Christianity and Classical Culture* (London: Oxford University Press, 1974), pp. 34–35.

111. *Roman Civilization*, vol. 11, Naphtali Lewis and Meyer Reinhold, ed. (New York: Columbia University Press, 1967), p. 573.

112. R. MacMullen, *Roman Government's Response to Crises* (1976) as quoted by Robin Lane Fox, *Pagans and Christians* (New York: Alfred A. Knopf, 1987), p. 64.

113. J. P. V. D. Balsdon, *Life and Leisure in Ancient Rome* (London: Bodley Head, 1969), p. 144.

114. *Oslo Papyrus* No. 6 (select *Papyri* No. 199) as quoted in *Roman Civilization*, vol. 11, p. 409.

115. *What the Church Fathers Say About . . .* , vol. 1, George Grube, ed. (Minneapolis: Light and Life Publishing, 1996), p. 163.

116. *Ibid.*

117. *Roman Civilization*, vol. 11, p. 298.

118. *Ibid.*, pp. 568–569.

119. *The Early Church*, volume 1, Hubert Jedin, ed., English translation by John Dolan (New York: Crossroad Publishing Company, 1965), p. 22.

120. *Roman Civilization*, vol. 2, pp. 479–480.

121. *Encyclopaedia Britannica*, 1978, vol. 2, p. 641A.

122. Shoshanah Feher, "Who Holds the Cards? Women and New Age Astrology," in *Perspectives on the New Age*, pp. 187–188.

123. *Taurus*, Third Quarter of 2000 (American Mini Mags, Inc.: Boca Raton, Florida), pp. 4, 7.

124. Ron Rhodes, *The Culting of America* (Eugene, Oregon: Harvest House Publishers, 1994), pp. 85–86.

125. *Encyclopaedia Britannica*, 1978, vol. 2, p. 641B.

126. Seneca, *Natural Questions* III. Preface. 10–17 as quoted in *Roman Civilization*, vol. 2, p. 255.

127. *Epicurus et al*, Vatica sayings, www.creative net/~epicurus/vatican.

128. Cochrane, p. 37.

129. *Ibid.*, p. 165.

130. Minucius Felix *Octavius* vi, xxiii. 1–4, as quoted in *Roman Civilization,* vol. 2, p. 574.

131. Michael Grant, *History of Rome* (New York: Charles Scribner and Sons, 1978), p. 332.

132. Moses Hadas, *Imperial Rome* (New York: Time Life Books, 1965), p. 127.

133. *Encyclopaedia Britannica,* 1978, vol. 15, p. 604.

134. H. Daniel-Rops, *The Church of the Apostles and Martyrs* (London: J. M. Dent and Sons, 1960), p. 327.

135. *Ibid.*, p. 328.

136. Alvin Toffler, *Future Shock* (New York: Random House, 1970), p. 398.

137. *Ibid.*, p. 13.

138. Michael Whelton, *The Pearl* (Salisbury, Massachusetts: Regina Orthodox Press, 1999), p. 185.

139. *The Report,* December 20, 1999, p. 39.

140. *What the Church Fathers Say About . . . ,* vol. 1 (Minneapolis, Minnesota: Light and Life Publishing, 1996), p. 167.

141. James Webb, *The Occult Underground* (LaSalle, Illinois: Library Press, 1974), p. 82.

142. Peter Washington, *Madame Blavatsky's Baboon* (London: Secker & Warburg, 1993), pp. 26, 41.

143. Marion Meade, *Madame Blavatsky: The Woman behind the Myth* (New York: G. P. Putam's Sons, 1980), p. 21.

144. *Ibid.*, p. 25.

145. As cited in Meade, pp. 38–39.

146. John Ward Montgomery, *Principalities and Powers: The World of the Occult* (Minneapolis, Minnesota: Bethany Fellowship, 1973), p. 26.

147. Meade, p. 41.

148. Sylvia Cranston, *The Extraordinary Life and Influence of Helena Blavatsky* (New York: G. P. Putnam's Sons, 1993), p. 29.

149. *Ibid.*, p. 36.

150. Meade, p. 91.

151. Washington, pp. 31–32.

152. *Ibid.*, pp. 32–33.

153. Meade, p. 70.

154. Washington, p. 33.

155. *Ibid.*, p. 51.

156. Bret E. Carroll, *Spiritualism in Antebellum America* (Bloomington and Indianapolis, Indiana: Indiana University Press, 1997), p. 1.

157. Webb, p. 11.

158. Carroll, pp. 2–3.

159. Webb, p. 16.

160. *Ibid.*, p. 17.

161. *Ibid.*, p. 18.

162. John Keegan, *The First World War* (Vintage Canada, 2000), p. 289.

163. Michael Coren, *Conan Doyle* (Toronto: Stoddart Publishing Co., Ltd., 1995), p. 4.

164. C. P. Stacey, *A Very Double Life – The Private World of Mackenzie King* (Toronto: Macmillan Company, 1976), p. 198.

165. *Ibid.*, p.199.

166. *Ibid.*, p. 196.

167. Cited in H. Wayne House, *Charts of Cults, Sects, and Religious Movements* (Grand Rapids, Michigan: Zondervan Publishing House, 2000), p. 177.

168. J. Gordon Melton, "New Thought and the New Age," in *Perspectives on the New Age*, p. 21.

169. *Encyclopaedia Britannica*, 1972, vol. 21, p. 43.

170. *Dancing in the Light*, p. 267.

171. *Hamlet*, Act 3, Scene 1, verse 56.

172. Michael F. Brown, *The Channeling Zone: American Spirituality in an Anxious Age* (Cambridge, Massachusetts: Harvard University Press, 1997), p. 65.

173. Joy E. Esberey, *Knight of the Holy Spirit* (Toronto: University of Toronto Press, 1980), p. 126.

174. James Webb, *The Occult Establishment* (LaSalle, Illinois: Open Court, 1976), p. 161.

175. Giovanni Filoramo, translated by Anthony Alcock, *A History of Gnosticism* (Cambridge, Massachusetts: Basil Blackwell Ltd., 1990), pp. xviii–xix.

176. Frederick Coplestone, *A History of Philosophy*, vol. 2 (Garden City: Image Books, 1962), p. 36.

177. As cited by Filoramo, p. 101.

178. Peter Jones, *The Gnostic Empire Strikes Back* (Phillipsburg: P&R Publishing, 1992), p. 24.

179. *Ibid.*, p. 25.

180. Ron Rhodes, *The Counterfeit Christ of the New Age Movement* (Grand Rapids, Michigan: Baker House, 1990), p. 15.

181. *Out on a Limb*, p. 234.

182. *Ibid.*, p. 235.

183. *Encyclopaedia Britannica*, vol. 16, p. 1096, 1972.

184. Leo Donald Davis, *The First Seven Ecumenical Councils (325–787): Their History and Theology* (Collegeville, Minnesota: The Liturgical Press, 1990), p. 246.

185. Henry Chadwick, *The Early Church* (Markham, Ontario: Penguin Books, 1984), pp. 112–113.

186. *Encyclopaedia Britannica*, vol. 16, p. 1096, 1972.

187. Nicolas Notovitch, *The Life of Saint Issa*, cited by Rhodes, p. 29.

188. *Ibid.*, p. 29.

189. *Ibid.*

190. *Washington Times*, Nov. 27, 1987, p. E6.

191. J. Archibald Douglas, "The Chief Lama of Himis on the Alleged 'Unknown Life of Christ,'" *Nineteenth Century* (April 1896), as cited by Rhodes, p. 33.

192. *Ibid.*, pp. 33–34.

193. *Ibid.*, Max Muller, "The Alleged Sojourn of Christ in India," *Nineteenth Century*, 36 (1894): 515f., as cited by Rhodes.

194. *Ibid.*, p. 34.

195. *Ibid.*

196. Robert Schuller, *Living Positively One Day at a Time* (Revell, 1981), p. 201, as cited by Dave Hunt and T. A. McMahon, *The Seduction of Christianity* (Eugene, Oregon: Harvest House Publishers, 1987), p. 15.

197. *The Philokalia: The Complete Text*, compiled by St. Nicholas of the Holy Mountain and St. Makarios of Corinth, G. E. H. Palmer, Philip Sherrard, Kallistos Ware, ed. (London: Faber and Faber, 1983), p. 46.

198. Robert Schuller, "Possibility Thinking: Goals," Amway Corporation tape, as cited by Hunt and McMahon, p. 25.

199. *Christianity Today*, Aug. 10, 1984, pp. 23–24.

200. *Christianity Today*, Oct. 5, 1984, p. 12.

NOTES

201. Mark Tooley, "Apostasy at 2000," in *Touchstone* (December 2000), p. 46.

202. *Ibid.*

203. *Ibid.*

204. *Ibid.*

205. *Ibid.*

206. *Ibid.*

207. Phillip C. Lucas, "The New Age Movement and the Pentecostal/Charismatic Revival: Distinct Yet Parallel Phases of a Fourth Great Awakening?" in *Perspectives on the New Age,* pp. 200–201.

208. *Ibid.,* p. 189.

209. Lucas, p.193.

210. Cited in H. Wayne House, *Charts of Cults, Sects, and Religious Movements,* p. 239.

211. Lucas, p. 193.

212. David B. Barrett, "The 20th Century Pentecostal/Charismatic Renewal in the Holy Spirit, with Its Goal of World Evangelization," in Stanley Burgess and Gary McGee, eds., *Dictionary of Pentecostals and Charismatic Movements* (Grand Rapids, Michigan: Zondervan Publishing House, 1988), p. 1–19, as cited in Lucas, p. 194.

213. *Ibid.*

214. *Ibid.,* pp. 194–195.

215. Melton, p. 21.

216. Cited in Lucas, p. 196.

217. Cited in Lucas, p. 197.

218. *Ibid.*

219. *Ibid.*, p. 202.

220. *Ibid.*

221. *Ibid.*

222. Cited in Lucas, pp. 202–203.

223. Ron Rhodes, p. 166.

224. *Ibid.*

225. Cited in Rhodes, p. 167.

226. *Ibid.*, p. 167.

227. *Ibid.*, pp. 167–168.

228. *Ibid.*, p. 168.

229. Cited in Lucas, p. 203.

230. *Ibid.*, p. 207.

231. *Ibid.*, p. 205.

232. Cited in James R Lewis, "Approaches to the Study of the New Age," in *Perspectives on the New Age,* p. 7.

233. Bibby, *Unknown Gods,* p. 51.

234. Donna Steichen, *Ungodly Rage: The Hidden Face of Catholic Feminism* (San Francisco: Ignatius Press, 1992), p. 73.

235. *Ibid.,* pp. 22–23.

236. Madonna Kolbenschlag, *Kiss Sleeping Beauty Goodbye: Breaking the Spell of Feminine Myths and Models* (Garden City, N.Y.: 1979) cited in Steichen, p. 93.

237. Cited in Dave Hunt and T. A. McMahon, *The Seduction of Christianity* (Eugene, Oregon: Harvest House Publishers, 1987), p. 145.

238. Dave Hunt and T. A. McMahon, p. 138.

239. Cited in Hunt & McMahon, p. 146.

240. Cited in Hunt & McMahon, p. 145.

241. Cited in Rhodes, p. 169.

242. Redfield, p. 230.

243. Cited in Hunt, pp. 24–25.

244. Dennis McCallum, gen. ed., *The Death of Truth* (Minneapolis, Minnesota: Bethany House Publishers, 1996), p. 31.

245. Elliot Miller, "Breaking through the Relativity Barrier," *Christian Research Journal,* Winter/Spring 1988, p. 7.

246. Bibby, *Unknown Gods,* p. 67.

247. George Barna, *The Barna Report: What Americans Believe* (Ventura, California: Regal Books, 1991), pp. 292–294.

248. Reginald W. Bibby, *Fragmented Gods* (Toronto: Irwin Publishing, 1987).

249. Sociologist Bryan Wilson of Oxford University, cited in Bibby, *Unknown Gods,* p. 147.

250. Bibby, *Fragmented Gods,* pp. 1, 3.

251. *Ibid.*

252. *Common Ground,* Vancouver, Summer 1993, p. 47, cited in Bibby, *Unknown Gods,* p. 289.

253. *Ibid.,* pp. 121–122.

254. Cited in Bibby, *Fragmented Gods,* p. 224.

255. *The Oxford Dictionary of Quotations* (Oxford: Oxford University Press, 1980), p. 314.

256. "Deciding Whether to Discuss Religion Prompts Debate," in "Dear Abby," Tuesday, September 19, 1989. Cited in McCallum, pp. 199–200.

257. Allan Bloom, *The Closing of the American Mind* (New York: Simon and Schuster, 1987), pp. 25–26.

258. *Ibid.,* p. 26.

259. *Ibid.*

260. Henry Gordon, *Channeling into the New Age* (Buffalo, New York: 1988), p.134.

261. Cited in Rhodes, p. 169.

262. Shirley MacLaine, *Out on a Limb,* pp. 198, 209.

263. Cited in Rhodes, p. 169.

264. Alexander Solzenhytsin, *The Gulag Archipeligo*, vol. 2 (Boulder, Colorado: Westview Press, 1997), p. 615.

265. James Webb, *The Occult Establishment* (LaSalle, Illinois: Open Court, 1976), p. 161.

266. Douglas R. Groothuis, *Confronting the New Age* (Downers Grove, Illinois: InterVarsity Press, 1988), p. 202.

267. Cited in Groothuis, pp. 202–203.

268. *The Phil Donahue Show*, Sept. 14, 1987, as quoted by Gordon.

269. *Time*, Dec. 7, 1987, p. 68.

THE FAITH SERIES
By Clark Carlton

AN ORTHODOX CATECHISM IN FOUR VOLUMES

Volume One
THE FAITH: Understanding Orthodox Christianity

Volume Two
*THE WAY: What Every Protestant Should Know about
the Orthodox Church*

Volume Three
*THE TRUTH: What Every Roman Catholic Should Know
about the Orthodox Church*

Volume Four
THE LIFE: The Orthodox Doctrine of Salvation

from

Regina Orthodox Press
1-800-636-2470